Rock 'n' Roll, and Reflections

Benjamin Wrubel

iUniverse®

ROCK 'N' ROLL, AND REFLECTIONS

Edited by Moshe Siegel.

iUniverse books may be ordered through booksellers or by contacting:

iUniverse
1663 Liberty Drive
Bloomington, IN 47403
www.iuniverse.com
1-800-Authors (1-800-288-4677)

ISBN: 978-1-4917-9958-1 (sc)
ISBN: 978-1-4917-9959-8 (e)

Library of Congress Control Number: 2016909283

Print information available on the last page.

iUniverse rev. date: 06/23/2016

For my parents,
Arthur and Ruth Wrubel

INTRODUCTION VIII

IT'S ALL ABOUT LOVE 1

    ALL YOU NEED IS LOVE 3

    SOMEBODY TO LOVE 5

    HAPPY TOGETHER 7

    HAND TO HOLD ON TO 9

    PUT A LITTLE LOVE IN YOUR HEART 11

    I'LL HAVE TO SAY I LOVE YOU IN A SONG 13

    YOU'VE GOT A FRIEND 15

    BRIDGE OVER TROUBLED WATER 17

    CAN'T BUY ME LOVE 19

    SOMEBODY TO LOVE 21

    THE NIGHT: NIGHTS IN WHITE SATIN 23

    ONE 25

    DESPERADO 27

    EASY TO BE HARD 29

    EVERYBODY HURTS 31

    BOTH SIDES NOW 33

    SORRY SEEMS TO BE THE HARDEST WORD 35

    WE CAN WORK IT OUT 37

WHAT'S PAST IS PAST 39

    IN MY LIFE 41

    AMERICAN PIE 43

    THE BOXER 45

    TAXI 47

    AGAINST THE WIND 49

    RUBY TUESDAY 51

    SONG SUNG BLUE 53

    TIME IN A BOTTLE 55

    YESTERDAY 57

HOW CAN YOU MEND A BROKEN HEART...59

BEHIND BLUE EYES..61

LYIN' EYES...63

HEY JUDE..65

I STARTED A JOKE..67

IF YOU COULD READ MY MIND..69

IT DON'T COME EASY..71

THE SOUND OF SILENCE..73

THOSE WERE THE DAYS...75

HOLD ONTO THE PRESENT **77**

I CAN SEE CLEARLY NOW...79

(SITTIN' ON) THE DOCK OF THE BAY...81

HAVEN'T GOT TIME FOR THE PAIN...83

CAT'S IN THE CRADLE...85

NO ONE IS TO BLAME...87

NOBODY TOLD ME..89

DOES ANYBODY REALLY KNOW WHAT TIME IT IS?..91

CIRCLE..93

TURN! TURN! TURN!...95

COME AND GET IT..97

GET IT WHILE YOU CAN..99

HELP!..101

HOW CAN I BE SURE...103

DIFFERENT DRUM...105

JACK AND DIANE..107

DUST IN THE WIND...109

EVERYBODY'S TALKIN'...111

INSTANT KARMA...113

WITHOUT YOU..115

WITH OR WITHOUT YOU..117

WORDS 119

LET IT BE 121

LOVE THE ONE YOU'RE WITH 123

TAKE IT EASY 125

THE STRANGER 127

A WHITER SHADE OF PALE 129

CLEAR A PATH TO THE FUTURE **131**

WHILE YOU SEE A CHANCE 133

DID YOU EVER HAVE TO MAKE UP YOUR MIND? 135

WITH A LITTLE HELP FROM MY FRIENDS 137

LEAN ON ME 139

HONESTY 141

THE TIMES THEY ARE A-CHANGIN' 143

REFUGEE 145

YOU CAN'T GET WHAT YOU WANT (TIL YOU KNOW WHAT YOU WANT) ... 147

STAND BY ME 149

VIENNA 151

I STILL HAVEN'T FOUND WHAT I'M LOOKING FOR 153

STAIRWAY TO HEAVEN 155

TAKE THE LONG WAY HOME 157

DON'T LET THE SUN GO DOWN ON ME 159

IF YOU LOVE SOMEBODY SET THEM FREE 161

TEACH YOUR CHILDREN 163

YOU CAN'T ALWAYS GET WHAT YOU WANT 165

RUNNING ON EMPTY 167

AND WHEN I DIE 169

KEEP YOUR DREAMS ALIVE **171**

AQUARIUS/LET THE SUN SHINE IN 173

IMAGINE 175

BLOWIN' IN THE WIND 177

DREAM WEAVER 179

COLOUR MY WORLD... 181

HOUSE AT POOH CORNER 183

DO YOU BELIEVE IN MAGIC? 185

FIRE AND RAIN... 187

DRIFT AWAY 189

LONELY PEOPLE 191

THE PRETENDER 193

PEOPLE GOT TO BE FREE 195

FREE BIRD 197

FLY LIKE AN EAGLE... 199

PEACE TRAIN 201

UNITED WE STAND 203

WHAT THE WORLD NEEDS NOW IS LOVE 205

GET TOGETHER.. 207

MIRACLES 209

THE LOGICAL SONG 211

CONCLUSION **213**

Introduction
By Benjamin Wrubel

Wherever we go, whatever we do, we are surrounded by music. We hear it in the noises coming from the forests, through the trees. We are mindful of the wind as it howls its angst across deserts. We can't help but be aware of city streets as they come alive with the rhythms of the modern world. Some of these sounds are as old as the mountains, others as new as the latest technology. Whatever the case may be, music fills our lives. Some of these attractions are pleasant to our ears while others are distractions filled with disharmony. Each of us, including the communities from which we come, has found what is pleasing and worth pursuing for ourselves. Often the sounds mimic what we find in nature, or are expressions of the emotions we feel within. With our ability to create music, there can always be sounds to accompany us on our journeys. Some of these sounds we choose to bring with us from town to town, while others we decide to pass on from generation to generation. There is that kind of music that has been invented for special occasions, for those moments that are already filled with significance. There is a kind of music that was created for no occasion at all, except maybe for that moment of creation, itself. Then there is the music that's meant to carry us between those moments where there might not have been any music at all. This is the music that takes those silent pauses in our lives and invokes a sense of meaning or purpose into an otherwise empty space.

Music can take us to that place where dreams are fulfilled and fantasies never fall short of our expectations. Sometimes it even does such without words; classical music, famous for taking our minds where our bodies cannot go, is a perfect example. It makes us soar above the clouds and want to reach down to give a hand to mere mortals. When we want that larger-than-life feeling, where the entire world is a stage, then we pull out one of the Great Masters. On the other hand, Blues can touch the breadth and depth of our souls. It makes us look inside ourselves and reaches parts of our being that we never knew exist. Or we can choose Jazz, which speaks to us like no other form of music: instruments become people, notes become words, and every song will tell its own story. So, whether our life is full of drama, or if it's closer to comedy, we can find the right form of music to accompany it. Yet, even though there are many kinds we can choose, sometimes we just want…something more, even when we don't know what it is.

That's where Rock 'n' Roll comes in. Rock 'n' Roll gets its roots from many of the other forms of music that came before it. It combines them in such a way that the results are something completely different, and special. Special and different because it has taken the best of those other forms and reassembled them in such a way as to make something new and unique to be brought to the masses. The other variations of music excel, endure, and are appreciated by many; however, it's Rock 'n' Roll that has, by far, reached more people than all the other varieties of music combined. When we add it all up, we have to realize that this is no easy feat. It is only possible to have such a huge following when there is something of substance being offered. That substance (no play on words intended) is a connection to everyone, every day and in every way, that's what keeps Rock 'n' Roll going.

The heart of Rock 'n' Roll (with apologies to Huey Lewis & The News) is in its music. The soul of Rock 'n' Roll, however, is in its words. And, its words are what keeps it going so long and so strong no matter what is happening around the world. It has been over fifty years since "The Day the Music Died", February 3, 1959, but the form lives on. Old songs are covered by new artists. New artists come up with their own takes on old topics. Yet, either which way, it's the meaning that carries the medium through. This meaning can carry a song written in one era to have significance in another time. If this wasn't true, it would be a dying form, but, alive and well it is. And, in its essence, it keeps those who listen and take heed whole.

Rock 'n' Roll is the music that took generations from the sock-hop through a senseless war, through social strife, through economic upheaval, to personal enlightenment—and now beyond. The words from these songs helped scores of individuals cope with the world on an individual basis, with a global perspective, and ultimately with how they themselves fit into that worldview. These lyrics have become so enmeshed with the fabric and texture of our lives that if we were to remove these words the cloth that we call society would unravel. There must be a reason that this form of communication still exists to this day. Harmony, peace, and, most especially, love is that reason. With the world being such an uncertain place, we want something to hold on to. The words are what we can keep as our anchor through changing and recurring tides and storms. Remembering the meanings of those songs is what will carry us day by day.

"Rock 'n' Roll, and Reflections" is my personal take on the words from the music that is the background to my life. Its overriding message of love, peace, and harmony is one that has had an overwhelming influence on me. From the first time I heard the songs from "The Era of Love", to each and every new song with that same spirit, I respond. To this day, when I hear any one of those songs, I am touched, inspired, and moved in so many ways. It is this feeling that I would like to share with others. From the thousands of songs, and hundreds of artists, over the handfuls of decades since Rock 'n' Roll was originated there is a mountain of work to consider. I have selected the one hundred and one songs that have been most influential in my life. I still listen to and enjoy many others, though these selections have the most meaning and relevance for me.

When it comes to Rock 'n' Roll, there are a number of overarching principles. I believe these to be: *It's all about Love*; *What is past is Past*; *Hold on to the Present*; *Clear a path to the Future*; and, *Keep your dreams Alive*. In each of these regards there exists certain undeniable truths. These certainties exist whether we know it or not, or accept it or not. With that being the case, just being made aware of some of these notions is a step in the right direction. And, as a wise person once said, "life is a journey, not a destination". So, if we're not sure of what path we could be taking, knowing what options there are might lead us on the road we should be headed. Therefore, we should stay awake, aware, and open to our surroundings, situations we encounter and others we meet along the way. We should take this knowledge wherever we go, whatever we do, and remember the meanings, not just the words. As we do, those melodies and harmonies will be ever more pleasurable and meaningful. Our lives will be filled with the sounds, the memories, and the wisdom needed to move forward. This is the gift that Rock 'n' Roll gives us. So, as you live your life; sit back, put on a tune, and enjoy the ride…

"Three Generations" 1967

It's All About Love

The first, middle, and last thing in any discussion about the human condition is...LOVE. Love is the emotion that we are born for, live for, and die for. Instinctively we crave it, habitually we seek it, and when we lack love it can be quite destructive, both to ourselves and to others. Our existence is fulfilled with it, empty without it, and teetering between the two when we're uncertain about the status of our love. Love is the be-all and end-all to everything that was, is, and will be. Our lives have more meaning, satisfaction, and opportunities with love. The possibilities are endless when our psyches are tuned to, focused on, and reflected in love. When we surround ourselves with love our hearts sing, as with the songs we make part of our lives...

"In My Room" 1975

"ALL YOU NEED IS LOVE",
THE BEATLES, LENNON & MCCARTNEY, APPLE, 1967

"All you need is love"… nothing else really matters. There is no reason to what we do, how we go about doing it, and what the end results are, because these things do not matter if we try to live our lives without love. Over and over again the lyrics state that's all we need. Whether we reference this song to the times in which it was written, to the present moment, or to anytime in the future, it remains relevant. It is actually quite easy to accept this simple but prophetic statement of desire. Yes, there are many things we need to do to get through the day, even when we do have "love". Yes, there are, unfortunately, many people who get through their day without "love". Yes, "love" will not pay the rent, or put food on the table; though, all of these things seem to go easier if we do have it, and the case can be made for life being harder in its absence. We can debate to what degree it matters, to ourselves or in general, but, nevertheless, we do all abide by the principle that, in all likelihood, wherever we go, and whatever we're doing, "all you need is love"…

"In The Moment" 1999

"SOMEBODY TO LOVE",
JEFFERSON AIRPLANE, DARBY & SLICK, RCA VICTOR, 1967

Wanting, needing, loving, and finding "somebody to love", is, of course, the ultimate desire… The words that are spoken in this song are some of the deepest, most heartfelt pleas a person can—and a song ever will—express… These lyrics present loneliness and how destructive a force it can be. Whatever led to this feeling and whatever became of it is unknown; though to them and to all of us, at least it has been brought out into the light… The inquisitive "wouldn't you" turns into the declarative "you better" in terms of the definitive, finding "somebody to love". Every time we hear this song it's a reminder of how important love is, what people will do to have it, and what happens to us without it. The world is a better place when more of us are in love, of course, than when we aren't. We are better people, to others and to ourselves, when this is our cause and our quest. So, why wouldn't we all just want… "somebody to love"?

"Starship In The Park" 1976

"HAPPY TOGETHER",
THE TURTLES, WHITE WHALE RECORDS, 1967

"Me and you and you and me" is quite a turn of a phrase... Though, if we truthfully want to make an issue of it, in reality it isn't quite such a reversal. Either which way, the writer is saying the two of them belong together. Neither one of them comes first before the other as they both are equal. The playfulness belies the seriousness of the song and the meaning behind the lyrics. Joy comes from being united, in whatever order. It is saying that no matter what else is happening, no matter what other choices are available, a decision has been made. The future, accordingly, is not going to be determined by "how they toss the dice." Randomness has no play and does not factor in their game of life. They are the "us" versus the "them." There is no separating the two when choosing up sides. Where one goes, the other follows...and that's it. It is together, forever, no matter what the circumstance. It is for here and now, for then and there, and for whenever and wherever. There is no changing, rearranging, or questioning either their togetherness or their minds. This is because, it is quite certain that the two of them will be "so happy together." Now that's love.

"The Coast Is Clear" 1997

"HAND TO HOLD ON TO",
JOHN (COUGAR) MELLENCAMP, RIVA, 1982

It doesn't make a difference; who we are, where we are from, or where we are going…we all need and want the same things. That is, we all need and want reassurance and confidence in what we believe is true and who we believe we are. We need to know how and what we feel will be supported. We want someone to be there when nothing is testing our faith in sense of self and all is going well. We need someone to be there when everything happening around us makes us question our convictions and what we have become. We want someone there every time, and whether they're in all actuality there or not is not the issue. Yes, it would be nice for them to literally and physically be there. Though, it would be just as comforting for them to figuratively and metaphorically be there. In either situation, without preference or prejudice to the events of our lives, we want and need someone to be on our side. The journey that is life always seems just that much easier and more tolerable with another along for the ride. When someone is there, it makes all the difference that matters. We have been, we are, and we will be better off when we have that "hand to hold on to"…

"Our Back Window" 1985

"PUT A LITTLE LOVE IN YOUR HEART",
JACKIE DESHANNON, IMPERIAL, 1969

Yes, "the world would be a better place" if we all took this bit of wisdom and "put a little love in (our) heart"... It is so easy to forget that love really does make a difference. One ounce of love, to make a play on words from an old cliché, is worth a pound of forgiveness. Each day we have regrets for things we have done, other things we should have done, or things we never thought of doing until it was too late. Every day we have the opportunity to prevent apologies to others, and most importantly ourselves. With love in our heart we usually can see our way clear of those kinds of mistakes. With the right vision, we do not hesitate to do what we know is best and do not contemplate on what might have been, had we chosen otherwise. So, we shouldn't hesitate to ask for and give permission to others and to ourselves to be open to love. With love in our heart we don't have to "wait and see." The rewards are usually quite self-evident, immediate, and long-lasting. And, yes, believe it or not, there will be less conflict, frustration, and anger. More people will be nice to each other, open doors that were once closed, and reach to give a hand to those that need it. We know that if more people opened up their heart there would be less reason to close our eyes. We could see our way to bring equality, fairness, and tolerance to all people in all places at all times. Imagine that, if all we did was put in what should've been there all along. Then, wouldn't we say, that this is...much better? And all it took was "a little love."

"In The Garden 1" 2003

"I'LL HAVE TO SAY I LOVE YOU IN A SONG", JIM CROCE, ABC RECORDS, 1974

Whether we say the words, or sing them, or put them down on paper, or paint them into a picture, or however we chose…the point is for us to just get them out there to be appreciated. We never know when, where, or how the words are going to be released and what they will sound like, look like, or feel like. Though, we do know at least one thing, the why: these words must be expressed to have any meaning at all. To keep these words bottled up would be a terrible tragedy. The words left unspoken become our biggest regrets. Therefore, it's responding to the why that makes all matter of usefulness in this most important of things. It has no bearing on the consequences if it is winter, spring, summer, or fall. It is of no concern to any of the parties involved if it is early on, somewhere in the middle, or late in the day or night. Winds, rain, hail, or snow have no influence on anything about it other than maybe the venue of its occurrence.

The most important things that will affect the outcome of this recourse are the whys. Why we are thinking about that someone, why we are feeling that something for them, and, why we need to let them know that. So, however, whenever, and wherever we express it, the words can never come "out wrong". We must release the genie from its bottle, whatever the wishes bring us. Because, when we "have to say I love you," it is always right and must be released. And, being right, it can never go wrong as long as what we are doing is coming from deep down inside and would be worse if left entrapped. We know that going with our gut, believing with our heart, and expressing our feelings is being true to ourselves. So, if the truth is always better than a lie, then that's what must be said… "I love you."

"In The Midst of Winter…" 2000

"YOU'VE GOT A FRIEND",
JAMES TAYLOR (CAROLE KING), WARNER BROTHERS, 1971

Love is eternal…so what if the seasons change, the years go by, or life's circumstance have rearranged? It could be one yesterday or hundreds or even thousands of them since you've last seen each other. There are some things that transcend time, place, and all sorts of occurrences, consequences, or compromises. When one person is that close to another person they have been, are, and will be "friends" forever. This friendship protects, oversees, and connects the two of them no matter what kinds of distances separates them. When one of the two is affected by another person, dejected by the world around them, or infected by the callousness of the human experience, this friendship leaps into action. There is no need for a long drawn out explanation or list of reasons; care, comfort, and compassion are at the ready. "All you have to do is call" becomes the minimum requirement to elicit the emergency response system. In no time, that first responder will be at the doorstep. With minimal forethought and maximum effort, that lifeline will be thrown. Without a word, that best of all possible experts will know what to do and say in that situation. When someone knows another as well as that person knows themselves, well then…all of life's troubles are manageable when you know "you've got (that kind of) a friend."

"Tree Houses" 1996

"BRIDGE OVER TROUBLED WATER",
SIMON & GARFUNKEL, COLUMBIA, 1970

One of the all-time classic images of comfort is that of a "bridge over troubled waters"…we have all been at that crossing, whether in reality or in fantasy. We have stood there feeling helpless on the banks of a raging river or on the shores of a turbulent sea. The absence of calmness on the water mirrors our lives and can overturn even the strongest of us. We seek solid and dry ground for the assuredness and stability we need in our lives just to carry on. Without a way to get from a state of uncertainty, we may never overcome the sense that "pain is all around." Yet, as simple an act as having a friend to "comfort you" can dry away the tears. As these drops of sadness fade from memory, even the salty residue left behind can lose its meaning. Thankfully, "your time has come to shine" as your friend settles those waters for you. Slowly, your mind eases when you realize that you have a friend who would lay down "(across those) troubled waters" for you. That bridge, between what was and what could be, has no equal to it. That solace, to know it can span whatever gap befalls whatever situation, has no price that can be assigned to it. That knowledge, to be able to make it to the other side unscathed, has no words that could ever describe it. It is reassuring to be aware of such a one-of-a-kind, for no other, and no toll necessary "bridge…"

"View From the Top" 1978

"CAN'T BUY ME LOVE",
THE BEATLES, CAPITOL, 1964

As opposed to many other sentiments- "Money makes the world go round"; "Money is the root of all evil"; "You can't live without money"- it takes quite a bit of nerve to suggest that "money can't buy me love"… Who would ever think that there is anything in this life that didn't have a price? Is there ever a time that we would believe that anyone we met didn't have an ulterior motive? Is it possible to "want the kind of thing that money can't buy"? We should say that we're sure it's not only possible, but that it's definite and real. How do we know? Well, when it comes to true love, that's just the way it is. Diamond rings and all sorts of things can presumably bind people together; however, for true attachment, we do not need material possessions. We use the currency of love. It brings us closer to another human being than can be achieved by any mere item that sparkles or shines. Over time, those "things" lose luster and value- especially the meaningful kind. They're just things to which we attach the wrong kind of worth. The "things" that really matter have relative values that are both internal and eternal. These are the items that we buy with love, not money: they will show great appreciation and continued compounded interest for all time. So, if we're looking to go out for a sale, we have to remember that we get what we pay for. The best deals never come at a bargain price, and "money can't buy (us) love"…

"On The Road to Nowhere" 2013

"SOMEBODY TO LOVE",
QUEEN, ELEKTRA, 1976

The title of this song may be the same as another one that was discussed earlier, but now the tables are turned…instead of "you better find somebody", it's a case of "can anybody find me somebody?" The general plea has to be heard as it's spoken aloud: the effort behind this plea can be heard as wearing on this person's soul. Dying "a little", aching to the "bones", and praying on bent "knees" isn't helping them one bit. Trying "everyday", having no one to "believe", and losing the "rhythm (and) beat" sure isn't this person's answer. So, a question is posed to all of us who will hear their words. Freedom from this person's pain and suffering depends on someone not only hearing the words but also responding to the request. The message goes out with a sense of urgency, determination, and impatience for an answer to the question: "Can anybody find me somebody to love?" It is our job, our calling or better yet, our obligation to do so. The only question is: are they asking for themselves, or are they really asking for us? Sometimes we look towards others and find what we actually see in ourselves. So, we had better be sure that we're not the one in need. Either way, if it is them or us that have been diagnosed, there is a prescription that needs to be filled. If that is the case, for a positive prognosis someone out there hopefully is listening…

"Someone to Look Out for Me" 2002

"THE NIGHT: NIGHTS IN WHITE SATIN", MOODY BLUES, DERAM RECORDS, 1967

If we want love, we will ask for love, and hopefully we will get love… There's no other road than the direct one and no way of getting around- only through- any obstacles. If, in our heart of hearts, it's what we seek then we will make and take every opportunity to get started. Consciously or subconsciously we will arrange our plans and decisions to get us on that path. This sojourn will occur whether we have written down our thoughts, tried to explain them to another, or even bothered to admit them to ourselves. It is only when we let our feelings guide us that we can seek our fulfillment; we will ultimately feel this need to get going and it will guide us in the right direction. As this song states, in the end we will be "just what (we) want to be". Eventually, any letters that were unwritten, messages unsent, non-substantiated truths, non-rectified denials, and the like, will have to come to an end. So, what we need to do is speak loudly and clearly, and say the words to another- any other. Once the truth has revealed itself we can take that first step. Our journey will lead us to the right place and time. What we have to do is repeat what we have said not only to ourselves, but also to that person, and express what was actually meant to be said all along. We can then gaze into their eyes and let the beauty of our emotions be the words that come from- and touch- deep down inside. As we say "I love you"… then, and only then, will everyone involved know "just what the truth is".

"Sky View 2" - 1979

"ONE",
THREE DOG NIGHT, DUNHILL, 1969

Maybe it's "better to have loved and lost than never to have loved at all"… though, if he were around today, Alfred, Lord Tennyson would have to agree that being alone and rejected is no match to having once been part of a relationship. There are so many advantages to living and sharing your life; opportunities, appreciations, and alternate vantage points far outnumber those of going it alone. Making new memories and having good times outweigh the alternative of leaving a blank slate. Yet, when we've been left to sit there "just making rhymes of yesterday", we may not think so. It is, without a doubt, one of the hardest things that one may ever experience, feelings that any one of us would try to avoid. Though, "one" is both the way we come into this world and the way we leave it; therefore, the moments in between should not be spent in solitude. There are too many things that we could be doing with too many people for us to justify being alone. "It's just no good" to pass up on these times. It is within those "free" moments, hours, days, and years that we have a chance to not be that single number. We should spend our energy, during our wakefulness- and throughout even our dream states- to make sure of this. It is of no benefit to us, or anyone else for that matter, to have first-hand knowledge that "one is the loneliest number".

"Living On The Edge" 1996

"DESPERADO",
THE EAGLES, ASYLUM, 1973

How many people do we know that have built for themselves their own "prison"? Are we one of those people? If we admit it, there may have been a time or two in our past when we've started the construction… We may have even completed a stage or two of the project. If we're lucky, we scrapped it and cleared the landscape. Hopefully, once knocked down, these sites aren't easily remade. So, in the future we'll have to think carefully when wanting to lay a new foundation. We know that plans can change and corrections have to be considered at least once or twice. There are so many factors that come into play when drawing up the designs of our lives. Though, it's easy to be hard on ourselves during the process of making a life. It's just not so easy to "come to (our) senses" when we're hurting. If opportunity places things on our table, it's only natural for us to want what we can't reach- or what we shouldn't go for, in the first place. It's only common sense that, maybe, other things will make us happy and act less desperate. The trick is to figure out which is which. We often have to come down from our high horse and know that things aren't always going to be perfect. We can accept things as they are, and know that it'll be alright if only we open up our hearts. Whether we learn it the easy way or the hard way, we better learn it "before it's too late". Once the fences are up we better have already let someone in. Otherwise, we'll be locked in on the wrong side of the gate. If we want to turn a house into a home we've got to realize that "you better let somebody love you". Period! End of sentence…

"In The Quietest Moments" 2005

"EASY TO BE HARD",
THREE DOG NIGHT, DUNHILL, 1969

How can it be so easy to turn our head away when someone calls out our name? Why can it be so hard to take hold, when they stretch out their hand to us? When we come across a "needing friend", what makes so many of us heartless, cruel, cold, and without feeling? Haven't we all been in the situation where we were the ones in need of help? Wouldn't we all be better off if we were to put ourselves in the other person's place, at least once in a while? Couldn't we imagine what it would be like to be that person, in that place, at that time, and in want of aid? How is it that we don't yet know that we should care about "strangers, social injustice, bleeding crowds" and, especially, a friend in need? Where do all these people think they are? How are they able to make it alone in the world? Every one of us, at some point in our lives, is going to ask these questions, and hopefully come up with the same answer: empathy. No matter when it is, where it is, or who we are, it's just a matter of us having to figure that out. So, without a doubt, someday it will be us. We'll know when it's happened. Hopefully, we'll learn this lesson before such a time, and won't be the one asking 'how this has happened, and where is everyone?' Those of us who have already been there, know. Unfortunately, the rest find it "easy to be hard"…

"Bad Water Rising" 1996

"EVERYBODY HURTS",
R.E.M., WARNER BROTHERS, 1992

Before "it's time to sing along," we should all learn the words… We might think we know them when we're in pain and suffering. Though, we can't really hear what is being said when we're hurt and crying. So, if we took a moment and just a moment we might be able to listen. At times it may seem that we can't bear or spare even a second for this. Yet, at night, after a lonely day, when no one is around and it is only us there by ourselves we need to "hang on". In the quiet and the solitude the words will come to us. We don't have to have sung them before. We don't even have to know the melody. We might have heard somebody, sometime, somewhere singing them out loud. The words we can hear, if we speak them or listen to our mind's ear, are: "Everybody hurts sometime." It may not be easy to relate, it may be difficult to understand, but in our heart we know it's true. We have to accept it as a fact, that it is part of our existence, and that it is unavoidable. Only then would we know that "(we) are not alone". When we know that everyone must go through it, it makes it just that much more tolerable. When we realize that anyone who is still around has made it past that point, we can see the light at the end of the tunnel. So, no matter how much we think that we won't make it, that no one knows how we feel, and that it's never happened to any one before, it's not true. This is all a part of life and we must accept it as we hope the feeling is just that and it will pass. So, until then, we must be resolute and patient as we "hold on".

"Snow Globe" 2002

"BOTH SIDES NOW",
JUDY COLLINS, ELEKTRA, 1967

Even though the lyrics say, "(We) really don't know love at all", we just know in our heart it's not true… When we suggest that the meaning eludes us it usually means that we are aware of this in and of itself. Therefore, a basic understanding of what it is and what it isn't can be taken for granted. This being the case, whether we've looked "from both sides now" or "from give and take", we have actually looked. Knowing enough to see if it's an illusion or not means we are open to the truth of it. Therefore, what remains is fact, and we realize that love has the ability to "blind (us)". If and when the love ends, what we "recall" is not what is in plain sight. Rather, what we have seen is pure and without dimension, something that we may think we did not know. Though, without doubt, we do know because part of knowing is experiencing, and the lyrics of this song embody this existence. We are what we have been through and can't deny it has made us who we are. Whether we want to or not, we have to accept that we are here because we have been there. We are the sum total of all our yesterdays. And, everybody's yesterdays include some love. Whether we can or not, we have to believe that at some time in some place we were loved. It may have been the day we were born. It may have been the day we got or gave our first kiss. It may have been of our choosing or of fortuitous circumstance. Either which way, for each and every one of us, we have had love. Having had love, we know it, and, most importantly, it knows us. So, when we're not sure, we shouldn't worry about not being able to recognize love, because it recognizes us.

"As Day Turns to Night" 1983

"SORRY SEEMS TO BE THE HARDEST WORD", ELTON JOHN & BERNIE TAUPIN, MCA RECORDS, 1976

'What,' 'where,' and 'why' should come to mind when we hear this song… What, what, what in the world can we do that we haven't already thought of, in this circumstance? Where could we stand to make sure that "lightening strikes (us)" and that we're awoken to realize whether it's a dream or not? Why is it that we all know that "the hardest word" shouldn't be, but of course, is, "sorry"? We know, all too well, these questions and the responses that would truthfully answer them. Too many of us have been in a situation where trying to make another person hear, care, want, or love them is so sad it's almost "absurd". When the love has been so great, huge mistakes have been made, and apologies aren't enough for reconciliation, what do you do? When that kind of love between two people exists, and forgiveness is so vital to their combined recovery, with rejection devastating to each other's lives: What can you do? Where do you begin? Why did you let it get that far? Who is at fault might also be asked, yet, declaring that everybody's at fault- and therefore nobody is to blame- might be the better consensus. Then, there's really only one more question that needs to be asked: How do you dare take the chance to make it right by saying that one, and only one, word, "sorry"? You just do… because, even though it's the "hardest word" to say, it's the only one that matters.

"Make Your Own Shade" - 2000

"WE CAN WORK IT OUT",
THE BEATLES, CAPITOL, 1965

The Universe is a big place, so much bigger than we could ever imagine… Galaxies, stars, and planets all move in a way that we think we understand. No matter how much we want to, their destiny isn't within our control or grasp. Eventually, objects will collide, combine with one another or disassociate from each other or themselves. There are no ifs, ands, or buts about it. That's just the way things will play out. It's only just a matter of where, when, and how it will all happen. There's no "fussing and fighting" that need be done in this concern. So, if something as grand in scale as this must follow the laws of nature, then things more minute in stature have no chance. We transient, sentient beings would be remiss to try and commit any "crime" against this order. If "life is (so) short" and "there's no time" to make corrections, wouldn't it be in our best interests to follow the natural course of things? Do we have any right or ability to alter these headings? Wouldn't it be best to just navigate the waves as we come to them? Couldn't we do this together through our own cosmos? Need we consider adjustments that though wrong make us "think that it's alright"? Is it worth the risk of changing plans to know that we may lose our way and with it the path that our love took? Love isn't an easy road to stay on, but it's the one that's best to travel over. Love isn't a given, and it can't be taken for granted. Love makes mistakes, though it can be corrected. Or, as requires repeating over and over again for the certainty of its directive, we know, that with love guiding us… "We can work it out".

"Up In the Air" 2011

What's Past is Past

A common theme running through the words of the songs of the past... is the past. We all learned early on that we can't know where we're going without knowing where we've been. In that regard, we've also heard that you can't take it with you. Memories, stories, photographs, and artifacts are all well and good. Nostalgia, reminisces, recounting, and recollections can all paint a pretty picture. However, to truly move forward we must let go of all those things that weigh us down and hold us back. Yes, those thoughts and objects are the history that has made us the people we are today. Yet, we don't need any of those things to grow and to fulfill our potential. Instinctively, we know that everything we need we carry with us wherever we go. The past has gifted us the knowledge and wisdom to make the right choices in the present moment. Only those decisions, made with the strength and courage of this certainty can take us where we need to be:

"Life Is About Change" 1976

"IN MY LIFE",
THE BEATLES, PARLOPHONE, 1965

In our lives, the days, weeks, months, and years do pass by quickly... Sometimes it seems as though something happened only yesterday, but it was many years ago. Other times we imagine what occurred recently really did so much longer ago. Then there are times we know exactly what we were doing, where it was, with whom, to the last detail and exactly when it was. There are moments that we will never forget and others we wish we didn't remember. A memory is a memory, is a memory, and so on... Usually, we have little say in what we hold on to and what we let go. Try as hard as we might, this is one battle in which we can only hope to draw even. The reason being, as we may have already come across, is that it has to do with emotions. The more we feel, the stronger the connection to the event. Love and hate work equally well in this regard, with indifference being neutral. So, we hope for more affection than need for any deflection in our recollections. We try to recall all those "moments with lovers and friends". We know that the places we have been may have changed, "some forever not for better". Though, we hold on to, as best we can, the "affection" we had for those places and people. Rightfully so, some things stand out and we try to hold those above the others. Often times, what we want to hang on to the most are those for whom we would say, they were "in my life". What we want to do when we remember is to be able to respond, when we "stop and think", it is of those people and places. And, lastly, we want to end all reminisces with the thought of someone specifically, out of everyone we've known, someone whom we could conclude with, and recite, "we love you more".

"My Room, My Stuff" 1980

"AMERICAN PIE",
DON MCLEAN, UNITED ARTISTS RECORDS, 1971

We may not remember where we were when it happened, recalled the circumstances of how they were killed, or were even born at the time, but "the day the music died" changed a lot of people's lives and histories... When Buddy Holly, The Big Bopper, and Ritchie Valens were killed in that plane crash on February 3, 1959, Rock 'n' Roll and all that it influenced was changed and redirected in ways we could never perceive. The same is true for every event that directly and indirectly affects each and every one of our lives. We can never know all the ramifications of choices made by ourselves and others on our day-to-day existences. What we say and do is obviously a reflection and reaction to the people and places around us. We can never be certain how what we do changes our lives or that of others who live within our circle of influence. However, we should be aware and considerate of this as we make decisions and take actions. When we don't take into account that what we do affects each other... what results might be that "the music (won't) play". This could turn out to be the most or least consequential of the results from one's actions. Though, we would never want it to get to the point where something done by one, or to one, would cause another to sing, "This'll be the day that I die". That would be a day no one would want to remember.

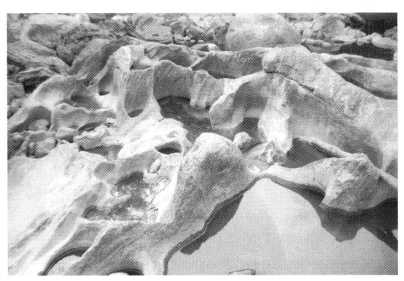

"Reflecting Rock" 1996

"THE BOXER",
SIMON & GARFUNKEL, COLUMBIA, 1970

How often have we heard but not listened? Haven't we spoken but not been received? Isn't it all a matter of nuance? "Such are (the) promises" that have been told to us and by us... Aren't we as guilty as others from telling, on occasion, "all lies and jests"? As we fight our way through this life we have battles every day. In the things we do, the places we go, and the motivation to stay or go, we are reminded daily of this. It comes down to a matter of determining when to stand and be counted or turn and disappear from existence. Either which way, it is our decision. We can "hear" what the world is telling us, and respond. Or, we can ignore the noises coming from all the others, as we "disregard the rest". Whatever the case, we will be reminded of the choices we have made. Scars on the outside don't cause as much pain and sorrow as those on the inside. We may never forget or recover from the wounds we can't see, in contrast to the blemishes that will eventually disappear. What we have to consider in either case is whether or not we were honest with ourselves, and, by extension, with others. Telling ourselves the truth is something that we can live with, as opposed to the memory of living with a "lie". The truth does not require a ring of deceit to be supported. To "lie" or not "lie" is an easy decision to make, when we know that we have to live with it. So, in life, choose to fight the lie...

"Just Like This" 1999

"TAXI",
HARRY CHAPIN, ELEKTRA, 1972

In life, regrets are things that we can never forget, let go of, or undo… When we know we should've or shouldn't have done something we find it hard to live with. No matter how much effort we put into trying to wipe out the memory of our inadvertent decision or correcting the ill-advised action, it just won't work. Time and again, when we least expect it, and most of all don't need it, we will be reminded of our choices. We will remember whether or not it's been "too many miles" or "too little smiles" since then. There's no magic or mystical incantation that can take away the past or rearrange the present. We could've dreamed, hoped, and prayed for different, but the future became what it is now. Pretending that it's not how it turned out won't change the past or its outcome. Getting "angry" or being "hurt" doesn't alter the events that did or didn't occur. Living with the results and letting go of what was is the only way to continue. In the "taxi" ride which is our life, sometimes we are the driver, other times we sit as passenger, but always we hope to get to somewhere we want to go or be with someone we want to be with. Any way we look at it, once we've made a choice the meter starts running. Having begun the ride, we know there's going to be a drop off point and a fare to pay when it's over. So, in the end, we should consider ourselves lucky if we've gotten to take the trip, been with someone along the way, and maybe have gone to some of the places we "asked for".

"Castle on the Wall" 1982

"AGAINST THE WIND",
BOB SEGER, CAPITOL, 1980

There's so much that this song says, it's hard to know where to begin… Though, we can begin by thinking about Don Quixote and fighting windmills, but that would be like "runnin' against the wind". We can consider the old saying that "we should never say never". Though, we would have to swear that having that discussion, itself, "never would end". We could talk about a "wildfire out of control", but by the time we were done so too would be the flames, with nothing left for us to do, or say. We could talk about wishing we knew then what we know now. Yet, as the song so elegantly puts it, maybe it's better not to know. We might discuss the importance of working to live, and not letting it be the other way around. We also could begin at the end, instead of ending at the beginning. Sometimes, when we don't have the right mindset, the journey is over before it ever starts. We know the part where the search to find something, especially ourselves, can take a lifetime. However, we all know that we were there, whether we wanted to admit it or not, all along. In all actuality, it doesn't matter where we begin or "what (we) leave in, (and) what (we) leave out". Truth be told, it's the living- of and being able to tell the story of our life that's most important. Mostly, it's about saying to ourselves- and being able to accept- how hard life is. It's alright to seek shelter every once in a while. As long as we're fighting the good fight, and living the just life, we know that no "wind" is going to stop us.

"Drift Away" 2005

"RUBY TUESDAY",
THE ROLLING STONES, DECCA, 1967

There are some things we come across that are worth holding onto at all costs... Those things are usually the ones we can't put a price on. They're not the trinkets, baubles, mansions, vehicles, and possessions of our life. They're usually the intangibles, unexplainable, unobtainable, unredeemable, and/or unrealistic thoughts we've had. Better known as dreams, we've got to catch them "before they slip away". Without them, what will guide us? Without them, what will inspire us? Without them, what will drive us? We all have dreams; though many of us won't admit to it, tell it to others, or even just put it into words. We all want our dreams to come true, though many of us won't do much or anything to realize it. We all need to live our dreams, though many of us are too afraid to do so. We will never "be so free" as when we reach beyond ourselves. We won't have "time to lose" when we stop looking at our watch. We'll stop "dying all the time" when we start living every day. Life is just a series of hellos and goodbyes, starts and stops, and beginnings and ends. At each of these junctures there are some things that have to remain the same, even though it might not make sense. The dreams must not change. Otherwise, how will we know which way to go when the road turns in front of us? Dreams are the signposts of our psyche. If we lose sight of them, we have to be careful and not "lose (our) mind", and therefore our way. So, it's of utmost importance that we hold onto our dreams as best we can. Dreams are the instructions and directions that will guide us and keep us safe, as we venture down that path that we call life.

"Meet Me Under the..." 1997

"SONG SUNG BLUE",
NEIL DIAMOND, MCA RECORDS, 1972

We've all known heartache and troubles…the human condition requires it. Without knowing the "blues", how would we know all the other colors of the rainbow? It's wonderful to be happy. It's miserable to be sad. Though, if we didn't have both, could we really recognize the differences life has to offer? To see the beauty that exists in the world, we also have to be able to look at those things which aren't as pleasing to the eye. To see it all and still keep our perspective does not necessarily mean putting on rose-colored glasses. More to the point, it means being able to see what life is really about, its true meaning, from every vantage. Suffering, pain, loneliness, and longing are all emotions common to one and all, at one time or another. It's how we deal with these feelings that determines how- and if- we move on from there. We all have our coping mechanisms, both big and small, to handle what life throws at us. Without some form of compromise of our actions, readjustment of our sight, or refocus of our energies, how could we get through our days? Everybody has their own method: some of us get quiet as others get loud, some of us get "weeping" as others might get "sleeping". Either which way, you have to deal with the emotions somehow, directly or indirectly. So, if you can't yet laugh about your heartache, then cry. So, if you're going to tell your story you might as well "sing it". The important thing is to just start to accept the circumstances, somewhere and somehow. We have to begin by mostly letting ourselves and others around know exactly what we're feeling. Only then can we start to heal, and "Funny thing…before (we) know it (we) get to feeling good." Once we've turned from looking at only that one color of the rainbow, we'll be able see all the others. What's so bad about that?

"Morning Bells" 2004

"TIME IN A BOTTLE",
JIM CROCE, ABC RECORDS, 1972

What a concept, "time in a bottle"… If only it was possible to capture time, how prophetic would this song be? Wouldn't we all like to take what is best in our lives and put it away in a safe place? Think of the possibilities of having that pure essence of love at our disposal every moment of every day. What joys we would have available to us, if we were able to spend "eternity" with the one we love. Imagine if we could make "days last forever" and keep "wishes coming true"? What a profound existence that would be. Realistic as we hope this could be, it is not possible. Though, our fantasies should reach where we can't go. Therefore, if we're going to aim as high as we can, we might as well shoot for the stars. If we miss, at least we'll land somewhere with the one we love. Wherever that is, it wouldn't be so bad if the moments of our journey were with that person we wanted "to go through time with". So, once we've "looked around enough to know" that this is the one for us, we should be on our way. We should do, we should see, and we should spend every possible moment as if it was the one that we were going to keep forever. However often and of whatever length these times may be, we should strive to make them reach our expectations. We can then take all that is wonderful about what has been and hold onto it as best as we can, metaphorically speaking. When we reach that place in the sky we were shooting for we can let go, metaphysically speaking. Only then will we be glad we'd gone through the trouble of making something that was worth saving for all "time in a bottle".

"Is That You…" 2001

"YESTERDAY",
THE BEATLES (LENNON/MCCARTNEY), PARLOPHONE, 1965

It is so reassuring and calming to know that we can "believe in yesterday"… We all need that time and place from where we can recall the moments when and in which we were whole. How wonderful it is to be able to go back in our memory and find that "place to hide away"? It was so safe and secure there and then that we hope the feeling lasts forever. We were able to venture out into the field of love because at that moment in time it was "such an easy game to play". How marvelous it would be if we could leave our "troubles" in the present and return to the past? Alas, that past and even this present are fleeting. As a matter of fact, before you know it, the future has already arrived. Now we can't go back and ask questions then that need to be answered now. Though, if we did not know then what we should know now, can we really blame ourselves? Yet, saying the wrong thing at the right time or the right thing at the wrong time cannot be undone. Wishing for sunshine when there is rain or daylight when the nighttime is too long will not change the forecast. Darkness and precipitation happens as they will and might, respectively. Time as circumstance does not stand still and frozen in the moment. Everything moves ahead and at its own pace. We can't play red light, green light, and one-two-three retroactively. There's no adult version of freeze-tag that anyone else will find acceptable. What we were playing at then has ended by now and we have to move on. Going back, as pleasurable as that would be, can't be done. Though, it was fun while it lasted. So, we continue to "believe in yesterday", while we live for today.

"Life Less Complicated" 1978

"HOW CAN YOU MEND A BROKEN HEART", BEE GEES, ATCO, 1971

Time heals all, though some wounds run deeper than others… The superficial scratches to our being may be unsightly, though we recover without scarring, even when damaging words accompany them. The penetrating lacerations to our substance may require medical attention. Yet, sticks and stones may break some bones that literally can heal on their own. On the other hand, devastation to our heart muscle has no known treatment. Therefore, prognosis depends on who's on call and what experience they have in such situations. Time may help, regardless of the depth and cause of the pain or suffering. Somehow, the "rain" doesn't have to stop for us to find some place to be dry and warm. Somewhere, the "sun" will keep shining, even if we may not see it today or in the upcoming forecast. A "loser" might someday win, as long as that person does not give up and keeps on trying. However, who could ever foresee and protect themselves from such a heart breaking? When we "live (our) life" and do what we "want to do" we don't think about those things. If we "could never see tomorrow" and were "never told about the sorrow" how could we respond otherwise? We're told from early on to live in the moment and make each day count. We believe in things by doing and seeing for ourselves. So, we come to our conclusions by experience, and nothing can take this away. We're given opportunities, and take chances to be able to say that we have done and we know. We want to try everything and say that we've been successful. A fulfilled life is one in which we get the most out of all that we do. So, why does it hurt so much when we've given it our all and someone wants to return what we've offered? Why aren't we told of that policy? Why isn't that kind of injury covered? Knowing the amount of damage that is possible, why then aren't we told, or ask; "How can (we) mend" it?

"California Dreamin'…" 1981

"BEHIND BLUE EYES",
THE WHO, DECCA/MCA, 1971

It's an awful thing to feel betrayed and unloved…it's something that we wouldn't wish upon any other. We might well up with anger, as the tears blur our vision; it's not a pretty picture to imagine the world through those eyes. We might cry out in shame, until our throat is so sore we can't speak; it's not a very pleasant thought to listen for voices that can't sing. We disguise what's going on inside of us by what we're willing to show on the outside. They say our eyes are the windows into our soul. Opened, they expose our true feelings for anyone to see. Though, what if we didn't want anybody looking in? What would we do then? We couldn't keep them closed forever. Even if imprisoned, by our own thoughts, we'd want to look for the path that could set us free. "Behind (those) eyes" we might be "sad" or we might be "bad". In all actuality, nobody would know us if we didn't let them peer in. Yet, we may not even know ourselves, if that's the case. When there's so much hate, does our fate come down "to telling only lies"? We may have dreams, hopes and desires. We may think that none of them have or will ever come true. Though, our glass may not be as empty as we think our "conscience seems to be". No matter how devoid of remorse we may think we are, it's just not in our nature. Just thinking about it means we care. We may, or, actually, may not have to be alone. That's because we would "never free" our thoughts of revenge to be acted upon. We hurt and we want to hurt back. Yet, instead, we sit and we tell others our story. We let them look into our eyes, even though "no one knows what it's like" to be us. Maybe if they had half a notion of what that feels like, they wouldn't do unto others what was done unto us.

"A Tree With No Name" 1997

"LYIN' EYES",
THE EAGLES, ASYLUM, 1975

The only person we can ever really keep the truth from is ourselves… We may believe that we are hiding these things from another person. Though, we then have to lead our life based on the lies that we've told. We might try getting around this by letting these slaves out one by one, but then they'll be our masters. They may be as few in number as one or as many as all the people we have ever known. Yet, the only person we're ever really lying to, once again, is ourselves. Let's just stop and think about it. When we tell the truth it belongs to us, and the whole world knows it. Once we've told a lie it owns us, and will never let us forget it. When it's out there we can't take it back. The lie winds up taking on a life of its own. The lie has to be remembered; it must be kept up, and tied into the truth that's around it. The truth then becomes less meaningful, because it's entangled in so much deception. So, we have to make the truth that much more than it is to compensate. Imagine how much work that winds up becoming. It takes a great effort to create what amounts to only a "thin disguise" to cover up our "lying eyes". No matter where we go, what we do, and who we see the result will be the same. We'll have to look and smile knowing that "life didn't change things". By hiding the truth from others, we've really only kept it from ourselves. The lie we've been perpetuating to them keeps us as "(we) used to be". How can we change and grow if we don't even tell ourselves what's real? How can we ever move forward if we have to constantly keep looking backward? Why should we keep worrying that the past will catch up with us? When will we finally realize that telling others the truth is what will set us free?

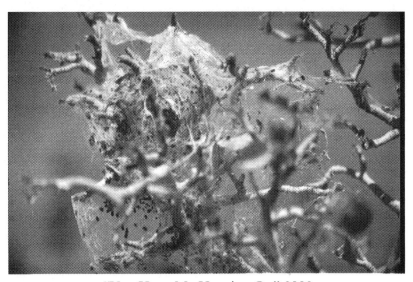

"You Keep Me Hanging On" 2002

"HEY JUDE",
THE BEATLES, APPLE, 1968

If we spend our life thinking about every move, it'll get quite complicated… If we dwell on what we've done or are going to do, it'll turn out to be a difficult life. If we look to the past and to the future for every present moment, it'll get very confusing. If we have to search behind us or way ahead of us to know where we're going, we'll never see what's right in front of us. If we second-guess ourselves or talk ourselves out of what or who may be best for us, then we're destined to a long, lonely road. Though, we can change all of that. Once we've taken the weight of the world off "our shoulders" and stopped playing "it cool", we'll see that it doesn't have to be that way. We can be confident in our decisions. We can live in the moment. We don't have to be "afraid" or "make it bad". There's more that can be done with "a sad song" then that. The world is not so complicated that we can't figure that out. We can use our senses, especially common sense, to know we can move past our past. We won't let what once was determine what will be. A simple thing like opening up our heart can rearrange these things. Our pain can be left behind us. Our future can be filled with happiness. It all balances on what we are willing or not willing to do. So, let's take a chance. Once we do, we "can start to make it better".

"Reaching For The Sky" 1997

"I STARTED A JOKE",
BEE GEES, ATCO, 1968

We never know what unexpected consequences life's actions have… Most of the time what we do will have the exact response we're looking for; we get a smile in return when we give one; we get a hand back when we hold out ours, or we get a hug when we open up our arms. Some of the time we do something that gets an equal and opposite reaction; we pull while they stand there pushing, we say black when they sit there thinking white; or we want to go out and they want to stay in. Yet, any of these scenarios can be predicted, reacted to and/or accepted as is. We most often know the outcomes of the events we've put into motion. Though, there are times when what we've "started" in no way represents what we truly intended. Sometimes, we do something that doesn't directly convey what we were thinking. Other times, we say something that isn't truthfully what we meant. Once in a while we show a side of ourselves that we've never shown before. Sometimes it's because we didn't want to. Though, occasionally it's because we didn't know it was there; in these circumstances, neither of us knows how to respond. Ultimately, questions abound: How can they cry when we're standing here laughing? How can they laugh when we're sitting here crying? Will we have to die for them to live? Will they have to let us go just so that they can be free? How are we going to get these situations straightened out? Why is it we ever thought that "(starting) a joke" was really the thing to do? Did we not know that everybody doesn't see the world the same way? Why didn't we realize who the "joke was on" to begin with?

"Just Waiting For My Ride" 2004

"IF YOU COULD READ MY MIND",
GORDON LIGHTFOOT, REPRISE, 1970

So often we believe that the other person knows what we're thinking… We've made all of our feelings, wishes, desires and dreams known to them. There's no way that they couldn't imagine what was on our mind. Or, just the opposite, we think we know what they're thinking. They've given us all the information we need to come to such a conclusion. We've reasoned out everything that they could ever possibly want. Usually, though, neither case is the reality at hand. More often than not, the truth is, we have no idea what is going on in another person's head. If we could truly read each other's minds, yes "what a tale (those) thoughts could tell". We wouldn't have to guess what the other person was feeling. We wouldn't have to wonder what the other person wants. We wouldn't have to ask what the other person needs. Yet, "just like a paperback novel", we might think we know how the story ends. Though, as in most good books, we have no clue as to even what's on the next page. We may think we know our part and the part that the other person plays. Though, life is never so simple that way. There are twists and turns, and complications that we can never predict. There are always other players and different scenes from all the ones we've imagined. There are separate story lines we haven't counted on and intertwining consequences that we never could've anticipated. There are words that needed to be spoken and meanings "between the lines" that are never read. It's when we're "trying to understand" what has been left unsaid that we often lose our place. So, before "the feeling's gone" and we "can't get it back", let's share with each other in words what has been to this day unspoken. Thinking what each other means without hearing what the other person has to say will always leave both people wondering "where (they) went wrong".

"Backed Into A Corner" 1985

"IT DON'T COME EASY",
RINGO STARR, APPLE, 1971

As we all know...life is hard. We spend most of our waking time taking care of the things we want or need to do for ourselves. Much of the remaining time we spend doing things we want or need to do for others. That doesn't leave a lot of time to just be ourselves or to just be with each other. Since that's often the case, we try to make the most out of whatever amount of time we do have. We try to get in as much of the "easy" life that we can. Though, as anyone could imagine, that's harder to do than it sounds. So, once we've experienced life a little bit, we look for its rewards. We use the fact that having lived, loved and laughed a little bit we know something about how to get these just deserves. Therefore, once we've paid our "dues" and sung our "blues" we look to move on to our spoils. We take all that we know, then we put the sad stuff in a sack, and we put the happy stuff out on display. In short, we try and "forget about the past and all (the) sorrows". We look to build upon what brings us joy and who might help us get some. In essence, we don't ask for "much" as we seek each other's "trust". It all sounds so "easy". Though, it's the simple things that we have to do that turn out to be so difficult. When we love and care for somebody we want to take our time to get things right. We go about in every which direction and try every way possible to get to that place. Yet, we know that time is always working against us. Life is funny that way, showing us all that we can obtain, but making the journey to get there arduous. Therefore, we try our hardest when we want things to work out. Though, as the song says, and we know, love "don't come easy".

"At The End Of The Day" 2008

"THE SOUND OF SILENCE",
SIMON & GARFUNKEL, COLUMBIA, 1966

Everybody wants to be heard but nobody wants to listen… We go about our business talking to, talking at, talking with, and talking without anyone there. We spend each and every day doing this and yet others often don't remember a word we said. We say we hear what others have been saying yet they often ask if we were listening. Neither one knows or recalls what the other one said. It's almost like we've been talking at instead of to each other. How many times have we reflected back on our day and tried to replay a conversation in our head? How many times have we wondered why someone said that they can't admit to saying what we know what was said? Were we actually "talking without speaking" or were they really "hearing without listening"? No one knows and no one dares to "disturb (this) sound of silence". It's a culture of having to say everything you feel but not feeling like listening to what anyone else has to say. Society makes it easy for everyone's voice to be heard but no one's voice to stand out. Everyone is talking all the time; at the same time as everyone else, and without taking the time to listen to what anyone else has to say. We say I hear you, but do we mean it, and how much harm does it do in the end. All the ills and regrets we have come from this lack of communication. If only we were educated on how to break these habits. Maybe one day we'll all "speak" and "listen" to "reach" and "teach" each other. Otherwise, the world will continue to be one very quiet place.

"They Built Cathedrals…" 1999

"THOSE WERE THE DAYS",
MARY HOPKIN, APPLE, 1968

The past certainly was a good place to be…at least, that's what they say. Not that the present is so bad. For the most part, that's what we say. Or, is it that the future holds some sort of unforeseen rewards? In every other part of us, that we admit to or not, that's what we all truly hope for. Yet, for some reason, the past is held so near and dear to us. We can't let go of things we know we should- or things we never should've held or that weren't ours to begin with. We hold on to memories that are sometimes no more than mistaken facts, faded photographs, or just inaccurate reflections. Were those days so much better than these? Are these days so much less than what could've been? Is the future really only for us to dream about? "Those were the days", we all agree, and join in with the song, but why? Is it for the obvious reason; "we were young and sure to have our way"? Or, is it for other reasons? Did we really think those days would "never end" and we'd "sing and dance forever"? Did we actually "live the life we choose" and "fight and never lose"? Or, was it that that's what we wanted and would do anything to get? Is it that we still want those things but won't quite go as far to obtain them? Likely, it's neither one of those things. Coincidentally, we've lived and learned since those days. Even if we're "older but no wiser" we are more experienced. With this comes knowledge and realization. So, we may have thought we know what life had to offer us. Unfortunately, if we're honest with ourselves, that's not most likely true. The only truth we know and should consider is what's "in our hearts" and if our "dreams are still the same". If that's the case, then "my friend", these can be the days.

"The College Life" 1975

Hold Onto the Present

Whatever it is that we're doing, wherever it is that we're doing it, and whomever it is that we're with, well, that's what it is… This may sound quite simplistic, but it doesn't get any clearer. Life is full of what-ifs, maybes, and just-in-cases. Though, each of those is only speculation of circumstance. We have had, do have, and will have lots of opportunity in our lives. Yet, the thing that matters most is the moment. We are in the middle of this space and time. We can't move backward or forward from it. We only have the present to work with and we should take advantage of that. The here and now is what should wholly occupy our consciousness. Wishful thinking will not change our situations. Imagining alternatives will only be useful in the future, if we're willing to act upon those thoughts, and take the present to work out the details. Otherwise, thinking about any and all options that aren't available right now takes us away from so many possibilities. Losing that immediate connection makes it harder for us to maintain balance. It is only when we are fully here that we reach our maximum potentials. At that point, we have control, not only of the moment, but also of both our past and our future. So, make the most of, take into account, and hold onto the present:

"Keeping It Simple" 1979

"I CAN SEE CLEARLY NOW",
JOHNNY NASH, EPIC, 1972

It may be darkest before the dawn, and calmest before the storm, but it's brightest during the day, after the rains have gone... The sky will eventually clear no matter how much rain, clouds, and wind there might have been. When that moment comes, the light will begin shining intensely. It will spread out in all directions and touch everything that stands in its way. On occasion, it will break apart and shower us not with rain, but with color. The rainbow that appears will not only brighten our day but will show us the way...the path it guides us to is one that leads away from helplessness and one that heads towards hopefulness. The journey it coaxes us to embark upon is one filled with joy instead of drowning with sorrow. As we "can see clearly now", the road to happiness and wellness lies just ahead of us. Once "the rain is gone" we can take those first steps in the direction of a luminous day. From the shortest to longest journeys each needs to start somewhere. No longer can we say "obstacles" are keeping us from reaching what we could not see or where we could not be. Our day will be "bright" and our way will be clear. One step will follow another, then another, and before we know it we will have put behind us those "dark clouds". No longer will we be forced to say we are "blind" to what is good in our life. We just need to hold on until that moment, when there's "nothin' but blue skies", and enjoy that "sun-shiny day".

"At The Start Of The Day" 2000

"(SITTIN' ON) THE DOCK OF THE BAY",
OTIS REDDING, ATCO, 1968

Wherever we go we carry all our yesterdays with us… No matter how far we travel we'll still only find ourselves with our self. It could be day or night, rain or shine, warm or cold, and yet even when no one else is there we may believe we're alone. We might have changed scenery, attempted something new, or tried to think about things differently, but it all comes back to us. Those thoughts that "nothings gonna change" and that no matter what we do things will "remain the same" repeat itself… All our dreams, hopes, and aspirations keep replaying themselves in our head. So, we find ourselves sitting by our self. Not because we want to but because we need to. We have to figure out why we have these feelings of "nothing to live for" or that "nothings gonna come our way". As we sit, "wasting time", we sift through all those things we've done, are doing, and hope to do. We try to rationalize how we got ourselves into this position. We sit there explaining all the wherefores and whys of the decisions we've made. We try to justify every move we've ever made, and guess what happens? We're still where we are, in place, in time and alone. So, no matter what we think, want, or desire… what we need to realize is that "the tide (will) roll" in and out again, and again and again. No matter what we say, or do, or think, it will continue on with or without us. Therefore, we can either just watch it go back and forth, think about not watching it at all- or we can do something about it. We can go out, wade into that tide as far as we can, swim as best as we can, and get to where we're able. Only then can we say that no matter what happened yesterday, we still can have hope for tomorrow, and we're sure of this because we're taking care of it today.

"Take A Stand" 1999

"HAVEN'T GOT TIME FOR THE PAIN",
CARLY SIMON, ELEKTRA, 1974

In life, we all live and get by, one way or another, in the end, by making our own decisions… We can't always rely on what others have to say, what others tell us to do, or follow their examples. Sometimes, the choices we make aren't based on what we need, or what we want, but on how we feel. Oftentimes, the feelings we have don't express our true emotions, but are reflections of what we believe we should be experiencing. Our limited pasts dictate the boundaries of our future. Though, each day we must make plans using what we know at that time. We feel the pressure to go on, even if we know not how. No matter what we feel, we must make choices. These decisions are ones of inclusion, other times they are of exclusion, and on occasion they come down to indifference. We know when we don't care one way or another about something. Those are the moments or situations that we don't give much time or effort to, and accept the results. However, it's all those other times in our lives that we realize we have to focus on, because of how much choices matter there. Learning how to determine what's important, "leaving (ourselves) behind", or drowning out "the noise in (our) mind" can make all the difference. Once we've decided what we have or haven't got "time…, room…, and need…" for can simplify all of that. Much of the time we come upon these conclusions on our own. Though, looking back on our lives, we would have to admit that many times these solutions have come out of necessity. Life often puts us in positions where making no decision at all is not an option. Lots of the time, we wind up leaving ourselves in a position of extremes. We find ourselves in "pain" and we look to get out of those situations. Alternately, we find ourselves in "love" and we want to navigate closer to its source. In either case, we could use all the help we can get. So, it's all up to us, in what we have or "haven't got the time" for, when we decide…

"Rise Above It All" 2004

"CAT'S IN THE CRADLE",
HARRY CHAPIN, ELEKTRA, 1974

Did we ever notice how "then" (future tense) turns into "now" (present tense) and turns back again into 'then" (past tense)? I'm sure we all have noticed this, but never really paid attention to it…the past and the future are the same: they're not the here and now. We're aware of this, from time to time, and that it's affecting this very moment for each and every one of us. There's nothing in our lives that this excludes, except our own beginnings and our own endings. We've all said, "I don't know when, but…" at some point in our lives. We've all meant the "when" to be a specific "then": time *and* place. Though, like everything else in life, something comes up. We're never certain what that something is, yet, if we've made plans, we can almost be certain that some unexpected thing will get in the way. It could be no fault of our own, everything to do with what we've done, or some combination of the two. So, what we're doing in its stead, oftentimes, isn't exactly what we had in mind. Also, as we know, everything takes twice as long as we had planned for it to take. Nothing ever goes as it's supposed to. As my Dad often said; "nothing ever goes straight." So, after all the twists and turns of life's events, it becomes later and later. Eventually, what we had intended to do one day has to wait for yet another day. Life is filled with moments like these, and before we know it the opportunity at hand has passed us by. The "then" becomes the "now" which becomes the "then", over and over again. The "cradle" turns into a bike, which turns into a car, which turns into a rocking chair, and so on… Unfortunately, we all too well know what comes next. Somewhere in between we have to make the "then" become a "now", because the other "then" may not come around again. The saying, "we'll get together… and have a good time" has to be made into the present tense. "We'll", a vague future proclamation must become "let's", a concrete present affirmation. At some point in our lives, we have to break the cycle of planning and rearrange it into the habit of doing… Otherwise, too many tomorrows will come and go, and we don't want to turn around one day and say, "it occurred to (us)…" We would much rather notice these things while there aren't too many yesterdays behind us.

"Out On Your Own" 1996

"NO ONE IS TO BLAME",
HOWARD JONES, ELEKTRA, 1985

We may or may not have ever heard about, thought about, or used the expression "everyone is at fault and no one is to blame"… This song bluntly declares to us all that "no one ever is to blame". It does so without mention of what fault might have to do with it. We can guess that it was considered, analyzed, and then eliminated from the equation. There are so many times in life that we want to place fault on someone else, or they want to put it on us, or we all want to turn it in another direction. Yet, shouldn't there be included, at least, a brief recounting of the possibility? Otherwise, we would have to question why exactly it's being left out. Has personal responsibility completely gone? Does individual accountability become totally unnecessary? Or, as we might speculate, is it something more like the opposite? We may want to accept it's neither and both at the same time, if that's possible. We can "want" someone, and the person may "want" to reciprocate, but somehow it just doesn't work that way. We can do everything right, as others do everything wrong, and we still don't get the results that we expected. Somehow, we can't make "the last piece of the puzzle…fit". Try as we might, we watch "(our) hopes go down the drain". All the while we look for solace and try and find comfort and explanation. Either which way, if it wasn't meant to be, then it's just not going to happen no matter how much we want it to. There are times and circumstances in our life that we do everything we're supposed to. There are other times when no one is doing anything they're supposed to. Yet, still, in each and every occurrence, the situation unfolds in unexpected ways. We or they couldn't have predicted any of the outcomes. So, were we wrong, were they right, and would any of that matter? Is there any way that things would have turned out differently? Or, was it a case of imminent results? Can everyone just go about their business and this is just the way that life happens? We may believe in this or not, fight as much against it as we will, but, sometimes, that's just the way it plays out. Though, we should keep doing what we've been up to, even as others keep doing as they have been, and just remember, "no one is to blame"…

"Knock On Wood" 2008

"NOBODY TOLD ME", JOHN LENNON & YOKO ONO, POLYDOR, 1984

Try as we will, we can't imagine everything that's possible in this world... If we give it no effort at all, maybe then we might imagine some of the things that we thought could never happen? Though, there are quite a few of these impossibilities that occur every day. Yet, there are other inevitabilities that, wish as we may, won't ever occur. It does not matter how much we anticipate or plan for the workings of our dreams, they still leave us wanting more. We don't know why life works out that way... Although, there are other eventualities that we have to imagine or wait our whole lives for. They happen randomly and inexplicably, but, without question or doubt, occur to us none-the-less. We just don't understand how this too could be so, while, all the while, we wish it weren't. We all know the saying, "truth is stranger than fiction"...then, reality becomes a concept that we realize should not be taken lightly. It in no way can be left up to day-dreamers and wishful imaginers. It's just too important an idea, and too powerful a concept, to be left up to chance. Of course, there are times in our lives that we want to be led by fanciful notions. Though, the day-to-day events of life are a time for us to be firmly rooted to the ground. If we have our heads in the clouds it's hard for us to see where we're going. We may wind up on a path that shouldn't be taken. There are some roads, believe it or not, that are better off left untraveled. What we need to be aware of is the possibility that we're living in "strange days". What we need to imagine is that people can actually talk without "(saying) a word". We have to understand that it's common that people love without "really (caring)". We have to know that with all that's happening, there are times when "nothing (is really) going on". Too many people are suffering and trying to be heard, and yet "no one makes a sound"... If all of that is true today, why do we ignore it? Why does it seem that most people have lost sight of what really matters? Have we actually gotten to that place where the idea of a thing is more important than the thing itself? When did the golden rule become the golden paradox? We're not sure when it happened, but "nobody told (us) there'd be days like these."

"Out Of The Ashes..." 2006

"DOES ANYBODY REALLY KNOW WHAT TIME IT IS?", CHICAGO, COLUMBIA, 1969

What is time? I know what the physicists would say, but what is it to you and me? Is it something that matters? Is it something we should be concerned about? "Does anybody really know what time it is?" We go about life looking at our watches and clocks, waiting for sunrise or sunset, or disregarding all semblance of time… We go about our lives marking the time, and counting the hours, or doing whatever we want without consideration of any form of limitation. Some of us spend every last minute measuring every last second, while others never start the count…which is the better way to live? Do we really know how to lead our lives? Is it better to "really care" and find "time enough to cry"? Or, should we not know which "way to go" and "where (we are)"? If it's all about semantics then maybe both philosophies are valid. Though, if it's about more than just the words, maybe one way is more appropriate than the other; if we're just going to "run around", not taking the "time to look around", then we may not have a concept of "what time it is". It may not be so important to know every move of every day, but if we don't get the big picture, how can we take "the next step"? We have to "see the forest for the trees"… and, in so doing, take all of those things which must be considered into account. Otherwise, we wouldn't get the significance of what we're doing, and most importantly, its relevance to others. It actually matters that each and every one of us takes enough *time* each and every day to live. Conversely, if we don't *make* the time, what we find out is that, in the end, all that's left is that "we've all got time enough to die".

"Some Things Never Change" 1976

"CIRCLE",
HARRY CHAPIN, ELEKTRA, 1972

Everybody knows, the shortest distance between two points is a straight line…though, when have we ever known a journey to go without deviation? Is there ever a path or set of directions that does not- or should not- have room for detours? It is these unknown, unforeseen, and unwanted excursions that often have us off balance. How can we predict side roads that we didn't even know existed? Would we ever consider making choices that take us off our direct paths? For all the plans, preparations, and precautions we endlessly make, indulging in every obstacle ahead of us is nearly impossible. The more direct we wish to make our adventure, the more indirect forces pulling at us are…we are swayed by changing winds, shifting sands, tempting oases, and alluring sirens at every step along the way. It does not matter whether these distractions are real or imagined. Each and every detractor from our focus and intent often leaves us wanton for guidance. Which way do we go? Every derivation from our course changes our forward progress to one that is lateral, or side-to-side, and, sometimes even, with backward momentum. What was once in front of us is no longer plainly in our view… With "no straight lines" in our lives, now all our "roads have bends". Where we've felt like we've "been here before" turns into a premonition that we'll be here "again". Round and round, over and over, we keep returning to the same places to see the same people. Is it that this is by choice? Are these good instincts, the best of intentions or just mistakes being repeated? Yet, with "no clear-cut beginnings" and "so far no dead-ends", is our life really one big circle? We should all say to ourselves, "let's go 'round one more time" and see…

"Life Is A Wonder" 1999

"TURN! TURN! TURN!",
THE BYRDS, COLUMBIA, 1965

For whatever it is that we want, whomever it is that we need, and wherever it is that we have to be…the moment is always upon us. It's all we ever have. The past is gone, the future is not yet here, and nothing could ever change the present. Yes, "to everything…there is a season". We can't deny that there's "a time for every purpose under heaven". From birth to death, love to hate, peace to war, and laughter to sorrow there is "a time". Though, is every moment predetermined? Is there no free will? Can what is to be done only be done when it's destined to be done? Are there only black and white, or do we get to shade some things in gray? And, if so, do we only get one chance at anything that is in between? We can reflect back on all that has happened to us during our lifetime. We can rationalize why it occurred when, where and how it did. We can try to wrap our heads around the thought that this is the only way it could be. If we could not imagine it to be any other way, then how would it be possible otherwise? We can peer into our future and make all the plans we want and reason why it might unfold as our minds have laid it out. Or, we can take all that energy and narrow our thoughts and focus, understanding and appreciation into the very present. We can make every effort and take every reasonable step to assure that the "time" is now. In this quest, we need only "cast away" what is burdensome to us, then "gather…together" whoever will lighten our load, and head unencumbered towards "peace" and happiness. Once we "turn" in that direction and "turn" down that right path, good things will "turn" our way. When everything is facing as it should, we'll know "it's not too late"…

"This Too Shall Pass" 1996

"COME AND GET IT",
BADFINGER, APPLE, 1970

Hesitation can become the bane of our existence…when we second guess ourselves it only leads to trouble. When we wait for the perfect time we find it often never comes. Delay can then become not only the root, but the extension to many of our problems… When we know what is right to do, if the moment has come to say something, or the opportunity presents itself to act, we should do just that. Everything that is ever going to work out will only do so if we let it. Our gut will be the best judge of whether the timing is right or not. It may not be fair or just, but planning doesn't always work, and often the best results come from spontaneity. Wellness of mind, body and soul many times arise from instant decisions. When we stop and contemplate too much, the moment often passes us by and doesn't arise again. It is when we fail to act and instead think about how our choices are good, bad, or indifferent to us, that we lose connectivity. This loss of attachment to the moment, to others, and reliance on the here and now can become disconcerting. Relying on things that don't matter or listening to people who don't care, as opposed to a holistic stability, will lead to our downfall almost every time. Only going with our basic instincts, will we guide ourselves to a path of fulfillment? Otherwise, how could we ever reach our own ultimate potential? So, when we're asked to "make up (our) mind fast" we should listen. We already usually know what we want, have probably looked for where we might find it, and often have been subconsciously guiding ourselves in the right direction toward it. So, when we're told to "come and get it", we shouldn't hesitate. Everything up until that point, including but not limited to our gut, will help us sort through whether there's "a catch" or not. So, we've got to go with our heart and do what is right and best for us. Making our way in life is a delicate balance between when and when not to, because, as we all know, time and opportunity are "going fast"…

"Any Second Now" 2004

"GET IT WHILE YOU CAN",
JANIS JOPLIN, COLUMBIA, 1971

Today is all we ever have…yesterday has come, and by now, is long gone…tomorrow never quite gets here, because, as we all know, it always and forever will become today…so, we shouldn't hope for tomorrow to be the day we want today to be. We should take today and make it the tomorrow that may never come, or the yesterday that never happened. You never know, as the song says, "we may not be here tomorrow". And, yesterday cannot be relived, as my Mom would often say…"there's nothing we can do about it". Therefore, we should take that all-too-frequently stated *maybe* and turn it into a not-said-often-enough *definitely*. We would only have to make a few subtle changes. We could turn any *what-if* and make it become a *why-not*. Eventually, every tomorrow that will become a today can be as a yesterday that was well-lived. Today is the only day we get things done. Today we see all the possibilities life has to offer. Today we don't "turn (our) back on love". Today we say we're going to "get it, want it, hold it, (and) need it". Today we're going to forget about all the yesterdays that were nightmares. Today we're going to hold off all our tomorrows that may scare us into forgetting our hopes and dreams. Today we're going to let go of our wishful thinking and stop holding onto the past. Today we're going to encompass the world with one thought. Today there's only one thing on our agenda. Today we're going to live for the moment. With all our effort and energy, we're going to make the most of today. With all of our will and perseverance, we're not going to let anything get in our way. With all of this in mind, we'll take it to the heart, because today we will "get it while (we) can".

"Leave Only Footprints" 2002

"HELP!",
THE BEATLES, PARLOPHONE, 1965

Honesty is one of the hardest policies to maintain…it's not just that it's difficult when dealing with others, but mostly it's difficult when considering ourselves. If, and when, we can admit to ourselves the truths of our life, we are always much better off. If, and when, we can admit to others the truths of our life, they, too, are better off. If- as always, being the biggest variable in the equation- things are not the way we would like them to be, if the people that we are with are not the ones we want to be with, if the things we are doing we really would rather not be doing, then we ought to own up to it. It takes a big person to face up to this little word, *If*. It means taking the stance that we need change, that change is not happening on its own, and that if something is going to happen it will only do so with some "help". "Help" isn't always a thing that we can provide for ourselves. We often need someone else to be there; to have our "feet back on the ground" we sometimes need another person to get us there. Many times we don't need to look far, because just as we're about to fall, we forget that we're not really ever alone. Good friends will know instinctively when we're "feeling down". They will know intuitively that "being around" is what we need of them. And, most importantly, they are ready for us when we are most in need of that helping hand. As life changes and our relationship to others and our-selves hang in the balance, it is never a sign of weakness to turn to that someone else. It is inevitable that we must reconcile with the world around us for what we must do. And, whether or not it is within our nature to do so, we must be open to the possibilities. The need for assistance is never an indicator of inability, or frailty, or lack of knowledge, or lack of will, but one of honesty. So, being honest to our-selves is just as valuable as being honest to the people who receive the request… Therefore, when we need to, we should draw up some courage, swallow some pride, and ask "won't you please, please help"…

"In The Midst Of Summer…" 2007

"HOW CAN I BE SURE",
THE RASCALS, ATLANTIC, 1967

The only certainty in life is uncertainty…the uncertainty in life is that you can never be sure. Though, maybe we should have started off by saying, *never say never*? With that being said, we might be sure about some things… We might be sure about what we know? We might be sure about what we feel? We might be sure that we know how others feel about us? We see it's all about looking at what is around us. We have to know where we stand, where we fit in, and who fits in with us. We have to use all of our senses, especially that least common of all of our senses: common sense. Common sense will tell us to open up our eyes and ears. Common sense will tell us what we see and hear, and whether it's real or not, and whether we can trust it. Yet, common sense will fail us as soon as we begin to question it. If we have to ask what's right in front of us, then we have no business even being there. When the words "how can (we) be sure" come out of our mouths, maybe we should turn around, or "upside down"? If we don't know "how's the weather", maybe we should stick our heads out the window? Either which way, if we want to "really… know" then let's take a moment. We'll take the time to make sense of where we are, who's with us, and whether we belong together, or not. We're sure that we'll be sure when we're sure where we stand. "In a world that's constantly changing" there's only one way to know where we're going to go. It's once we know where we've been, that we can know where we are now. And, knowing where we are now is the only predictor of where we might be in the future. Of this, and of what we say, to all others, and to our selves, is what we don't have to be certain of…because, we're "sure".

"From Any Angle" 2011

"DIFFERENT DRUM",
THE STONE PONEYS, CAPITOL, 1967

In the cities, in the towns, and in the villages of the world the rhythms of life are not the same…even within the same locality there are always harmonious and disharmonious beats. Our pace, their pace, and the pace of those we don't know can sometimes mesh beautifully- and other times, clash horrifically. That is not to say that these are the only cases that exists, those of extremes; we know that, on occasion, there is an intermingling of sounds that fade in and out, the melody of lives…it is these occurrences that catch us off guard. We get lost in other's rhythms and lose track of our own. We find ourselves looking, though without seeing "the forest for the trees". At that moment it may be alright, but then we must decide, is this the song we want to play today, tomorrow, and forever? Are these the words of "love" we want to say to only one, never any other? Can it be that the sound we hear, even though it appears to be the same, is actually, to each of us, that of a "different drum"? What would be the case if we let go of each other's "reins" and see which way each of us went? This world is a very large place when there's happiness and laughter, with no walls to box us in. Yet, this world is a very small place when there's "crying and grieving", with what appears to be no way out. So, sometimes to get the big picture we have to step back. Separation is a good thing when it gives us the chance to see and hear what is really out there… Once in a while, we might actually notice that it was somebody else's beat that we were listening to, and that we have to go out and find our own rhythm.

"Sky Echo" 1998

"JACK AND DIANE",
JOHN (COUGAR) MELLENCAMP, RIVA, 1982

"Hold on to sixteen as long as (we) can" are words to live by, if we must…though, for most of us, they are words that will stifle and suffocate our lives. The harder we hold on to something, the more it cuts off our circulation, and the sooner we'll have to let go of it anyway. It's good to stay young at heart, but we know we can't stay young forever…at times like those, when we question our youth and our ability to stay vital, it would help to remember the old adage: that we should go through this world with child-like curiosity, while avoiding situations which would lead us to remain childish forever. It can't be clearer than that: everyone has to grow up. It's not that we can't have fun, but we have to be responsible. It's not that we can't enjoy what we're doing, but we must work to live. It's not that we can't hold onto pleasant memories, we just can't keep trying to relive them…as the song states: "life goes on, long after the thrill of living is gone". We have to hold onto the feelings that we had and let those carry us through… We, as well, may have been there, done that, and repeated, but that doesn't mean we should give up the hope of being happy again. There are new opportunities, new experiences, and new adventures all the time. What we have to do is look at each moment as a possibility for such. We can't think back to what was, how it went before, and that it might never be the same again; that's just insanity… We have to take each moment, each opportunity, and each person we meet as just that- here and now, not there and then. There will always be similarities. Yet, there will always be differences. As "changes come around", we must respond to each and every one of these as unique occurrences. This is what differentiates us from children and what "makes us women and men".

"Beauty Is In…" 2007

"DUST IN THE WIND",
KANSAS, KIRSHNER, 1977

Earth, fire, water, and air were once considered the four basic elements of life…we now know that there is more to it than that. Though, if we take the elements as a metaphor, we can find them, at hand, even in modern life: We are born of the earth, we sometimes have fire within us, and we need the water to cool us off, lest our "dreams" burn too hotly and go up in smoke. To avoid our aspirations becoming "dust in the wind", we have to be fully present in every moment. If we "close (our) eyes", before we know it, the "moment's gone". So, to not lose hope for our future and to avoid relying too heavily on our past, we have to exist totally in the here and now. It may be the "same old song", but even a drop of water has a chance to be alive… That "drop of water in an endless sea" we may think of as one of many. That drop is life, because without water, we all know, there would be no life on this Earth, born of fire and wind. Yet, if a single drop gets enough energy it can raise above all the other drops and escape to the clouds. Its journey up high may take it far and carry it wide from its course. If it gets tired of being alone it can relax and join the rest that have gone back to the ground. Without any hope or inspiration it may freeze and become solid, not having a snowball's chance to move on its own. Yet, with a little help from earth, fire, or air that frozen water can go on living. With a little hope or motivation, it can thaw out and start the cycle again. This story can go on endlessly- at least we hope so. Though, if "nothing lasts forever", who is to say that drop of water doesn't have a chance, or a right, to live for now? Isn't it possible that a single drop may have a full life enjoying many oceans of moments on the way? The four basic elements couldn't disagree…all things considered.

"Good Fences…" 2000

"EVERYBODY'S TALKIN'",
HARRY NILSSON, RCA RECORDS, 1968

There are times when we hear every word that is spoken, yelled, or whispered… There are times when others hear every word, in whatever form it has come out, that we have said. Though, for the most part, those times are the exception, not the rule. Most of the time we are actually only hearing most, some, or none of what was said…that is just about the same amount that others hear of what has come out of our mouths. Yet, the truth is we almost always admit to hearing more or less than others say they have spoken. And, others could be counted on for pretty much the same thing. That's probably a good thing…if we heard everything that everyone else said, that would just be too overwhelming. If others heard everything that we said, that would just be too compromising. Everyone would be inundated with words and thoughts, sayings and remembering, hopes and feelings…no one could ever hear what others have to say. No one would then have the time to even listen to themselves. What a shame and pity that would be…without listening to what anyone, including themselves, has to say, how could anyone know what was thought or what to think? Although, if everyone went about their lives listening to themselves and all others, then would we be living our own lives? If "everybody's talking", can we "hear a word they're saying"? If nobody's listening, how are we going to hear "the echoes of (our) minds"? Speak only after being spoken to. Listen only after being heard. If we don't do those things it will be like we are lost in a jungle or the desert, with not another person around. Meanwhile, we may be in the middle of a city with a million people in every direction we look. Though, if we "can't see their faces" they probably can only see "the shadows of (our) eyes". So, before our interactions come down to "stopping" and "staring", why don't we look and listen? Hopefully, everyone else will do the same. Otherwise, we might believe, it's time to get on a bus and go somewhere else…

"Into The Shadows" 1996

"INSTANT KARMA",
JOHN LENNON, APPLE, 1970

We can never really know everything…that's just the way it has been, it is, and it will always be. From the beginning of time to the end of days…we are born, we live, and then we die, unknowing all the facts. When we're young we just want to take it all in. As we get older we think we don't need any more. Though, as we number our days, it seems we know less and less. It's not that we aren't trying. It's that we learn all our lives and, yet, we die stupid. How could life teach us so many things and still have so much more for us to find out? Why has no one ever been able to figure this out? Is it that there are so many variables that it makes it that unpredictable? With all its twists and turns, how could we ever prepare ourselves for every, let alone any singular, one of life's circumstances? Yeah, we could take all the right steps, make all the right moves, and still wind up in the wrong place. The only way to avoid the endless number of uncertainties that could arise is to be sure of at least one thing…we must be assured of being true to ourselves, or that we're being guided by our own principles, or that we aren't infringing upon anyone else's ability to do these things. If we choose to abide by these simple rules we can be certain of that. So, when someone comes to "knock (us) on the head" or "look (us) right in the face" we won't wind up having that person "knock (us) off (our) feet". Being in the right will help keep us upright when all other indications want us to be flat on our backs. When we hold fast to our beliefs, as the Sun's gravity keeps the Earth held firmly in revolution, we won't be swayed off our path. As the Sun keeps burning brightly, we'll "shine on" with the knowledge that here on Earth, we're all part of "the human race". Being "like the moon and the stars and the sun", we're all existing together. We all have rights and privileges, and living so that everyone enjoys them is what we should strive for… Therefore, we must "get (ourselves) together" before "Instant Karma" tears us apart.

"Cloud Painting" 1998

"WITHOUT YOU",
HARRY NILSSON, RCA VICTOR, 1971

What would we do if we had no more tomorrows? How would we live if we only had yesterdays? Where do we get the courage to say that we only have today? And, if today was too painful to go on, could we go on anyway? These are all questions we may or may not have asked of ourselves before... Luckily, since we're here today to read these words, we know that we have come through with some sort of answer. Yet, what would become of us if we went the other way? The answer may not be the one we want. The choices we have may not give us what we need. What do we do? No one can predict that sort of outcome. No one can give comfort to that person who has to make that decision. No one can guide someone else who is on that path, even if they've been down that road before. Everyone has to live their own life, tell their own tale, and make their own choices. No one should say to another- and we shouldn't say to ourselves- "that's (just) the way the story goes". That would be of little solace to anyone. Though, as "sorrows" can go, having love lost might have to mean "living without you". Yet, still living, having loved someone at sometime gives the courage and the wisdom, and hopefully the time, to accept that life does go on... Having given love in the past does not exclude the ability to give love in the future. The only thing it may be limiting is in one's ability to give in the short term. Though, in the long run, not being able to "forget" what just happened does not mean never being able to reconcile. Replacing downtrodden eyes with masquerading smiles may have to become a necessity. Yet, all the while, knowing that we loved so deeply must be enough of a source of inspiration to carry us through... As the pain encompasses our soul, the process of letting go must be replaced with the thought of holding on once again. This is true, even if the person is our self that we need to hold on to and look towards for support as we reach out. "If living is without" a certain someone, then living with ourselves and accepting the decisions that got us where we are today is the next step to living again...

"Where There's A Will..." 2003

"WITH OR WITHOUT YOU",
U2, ISLAND, 1987

Making a Life decision isn't easy… Looking for guidance, we don't often see what we want. Asking for assistance, we don't often hear what we want. Moving in any direction, we don't often get what we want. When we try to make decisions in our Life, we often don't visualize the consequences of our actions… What would happen if we did this? Where would we be instead of here? How can we justify doing that? When could we rationalize having gone there? Who could we live "with or without"? When it comes to that last question, it often becomes a matter of who would we be willing to "wait for"? Is the answer found in what we see ourselves, or only when we look into another's "eyes"? Does any of this have to do with magic or mystery, or is it all real? Can it be about giving or getting, or is that not part of the equation? Is it despite, or because of, something that we (or they) have done- does it matter at all? When it comes down to it, do we actually have a choice, or are we only fooling ourselves? If we've gotten to the place where there's "nothing to win and nothing left to lose", are we where we want (or need) to be, or should we ever even try? As we know, oftentimes no decision is a decision in-and-of itself. Other times, having our options taken away from us (by ourselves or another) is really what we needed all along. If we can't dictate the course of our actions, the outcome of our actions can be directed towards what is best. Once in a while we have to leave well-enough alone… If we don't decide, and if *yes* and *no* are equal, if right and wrong make no difference, then maybe we should act as if our "hands are tied". Sometimes we should lead our Life as such, and let decisions be made for us. There are times we have to accept what is, even when there's a contradiction. These situations usually resolve themselves, by themselves, and at their own pace. When we try to circumnavigate the issue, afterwards we often wish we didn't have a say in the direction it took. As a result, we should just be satisfied because, either which way, we're still alive…

"Standing Out From The Rest" 2004

"WORDS",
BEE GEES, ATCO, 1968

For ages it has been said: the person who owns the words owns the world. If we tell someone all the words, in just the right way, will they believe us? If that someone hears the words exactly the way we meant them, will they then trust us? If that someone then repeats the words they were told, in just the way the words were spoken, will they then accept them? If that someone then says they understand the words, will that mean they won't forget them? If everyone then remembers the words, just as they were spoken, in the way they were meant to be heard, who will own them? If we say the words to someone to express how we feel about them, isn't that enough? Do we have to own the words too? Isn't provenance of an emotion more than sufficient to make those words meaningful? Does someone have to own the world too? Can't words be as "everlasting" as a smile? Isn't every "story" begun and ended with words? So, why is it that sometimes words aren't enough? Words also aren't always the be-all and end-all when determining or defining a relationship. Words do help delineate beginnings, middles, and ends. Words can show pasts, presents, and futures. Yes, words are sometimes all of these things and more… Though, as we all know, other times words are a lot less… Yet, at times, words are "only words" and all that we "have". So, we use our words. We choose them wisely. We dole them out carefully. We speak them clearly. We proclaim them loudly. In any case, we use them all the same, because there may be no alternative. So, no matter what, it's the words that let the world know what we want, need, and desire…

"Are You Sure It's This Way" 2004

"LET IT BE",
THE BEATLES, APPLE, 1970

Some of the most profound "words of wisdom" that have ever been written, spoken, or heard are: "Let it be". What could be wiser, when all else has been considered, than to let things happen as they may? We oftentimes spend so much effort and energy to make things just right, that we're afraid and aren't satisfied when we believe something is just not good enough. The old adage "perfect is the enemy of good", says it another way: Sometimes you have to leave well enough alone. As hard as that may seem, as tempted as we are to do more and as intuitive as it is to know that we should not, we go ahead anyway. Against our better judgment and the advice of others we will, time and again, contradict our own gut instincts. That deep-down feeling, which we know is true, is at times the most difficult guiding force to follow. When we are right in the middle of our "hour of darkness", feeling as though we "may be parted", and seeing that the "night is cloudy" we don't want to hear anything. We wouldn't listen to someone, including ourselves, telling us what to do, even if what was being said was written in stone. It is at moments like those, where there doesn't seem to be any way out of our predicament, that no decision we make will be right for us. Though, if we only let it come to us, reason is just a hesitation away...at times like those, we must shut our eyes and let the moment happen; before we know it, "there will be an answer". We may not know how, we may not know why, and we may not want to admit from whom, but words that have long ago been heard, spoken, or written will come to us. The words will be clear, the message will be loud, and the voice will be familiar. As we once again remember what we should do "in times of trouble", and that is, after all else has been considered... just, "Let it be".

"Shadow Of Myself" 1976

"LOVE THE ONE YOU'RE WITH",
CROSBY, STILLS, NASH & YOUNG, ATLANTIC RECORDS, 1970

Today is every day! No matter where we go, when we get there, or when we plan to leave: on that day we will say it is today…so why not make the most of it? Let's take the past and leave it behind in some old box. We can throw a blanket over the future and not look at it just yet. Let's concern ourselves with only one thing, and that is living in the here and now. This moment will be gone soon enough. The next is almost upon us. So, as we contemplate what to do, let's not forget what brought us here. We're all looking for peace, happiness, and ultimately love. Each one of those things we come by just a little bit differently. Though, in the end, aren't they really the same thing? Yet, when we do uncover the future to see what lies ahead, we often times narrow our sights for love. On the other hand, we usually set wide enough parameters for happiness and peace. Funny as that may seem, it's true. We're open to all sorts of feelings when it comes to matters of generalized, unspecified joy. However, when we shouldn't be limiting our choices we're constantly closed off to options that will give us pleasure. Why can't we accept that we're not for everyone and everyone is not for us? We can't go out and meet the whole world, just as they can't come knocking on our door. So, when someone comes along and wants to be with us, and we want to be with them…we must remember it's better than being alone. The best advice we can get or give in this situation is to "love the one (we're) with".

"It's Not What You Think" 2002

"TAKE IT EASY",
THE EAGLES, ASYLUM, 1972

Without a doubt, another one of the best combinations of any group of three words ever put together has to be "take it easy". No matter the situation, no matter who's involved, and no matter what side we're on, if we heed those words we can't go wrong. Whether it is morning, noon, or night, it'll work out for us. Torrential rain, blistering sunshine, or a mountain of snow won't have any effect on the outcome for us. Sitting down, standing up, or even "running down the road" will absolutely make no difference to us. If we've got someone on "our mind", if they've got us on theirs, if we're both thinking of each other, or neither one is thinking at all, it winds up being good advice…the important thing is to keep on going and not to let anyone or anything hold us back on our way. Life moves forward whether we want it to or not. So, we might as well enjoy the ride. People will think what they will, act the way they want, and invite us into their world only if it suits them. So, we shouldn't be hard on ourselves, trying to figure out how we fit into their picture. All that thinking will only get us inside our own head, listening to "the sound of (our) own wheels". If we go down that road, that's a heavy "load" to bear and will just "drive (us) crazy". Therefore, we must take these words to heart, keep pace with our own life, and allow others in when that's what we want. Then we can follow the advice that will get us closer to what we need, in three simple words…"take it easy."

"Order In The Chaos" 1998

"THE STRANGER",
BILLY JOEL, COLUMBIA, 1977

Within the lives into which we are born, there are things we do not comprehend…yet we go about our daily routines, knowing what is right and what is wrong. We've lived many a day, and counted the years. We learned who we are and what it is that we do. We've made many mistakes, gotten some things right the first time around, and, along the way, tried to figure out what we like and how to make it part of our lives. On occasion we confronted adversity and determined how to protect ourselves. We seem to know our place in the world and how we want to present ourselves to others. Though, at times, we put that all aside, throwing away our own advice, as we "disregard the danger". Who is it that we really are? What is it that we actually do? Can it be that we "never saw the stranger" in ourselves? Why would we do such a thing? If we can, "why can't someone else"? When two people meet are they really themselves? Love will make us do many things. It makes us "share so many secrets", while also keeping others that "we never tell". When we look at what we've said and done, we often don't recognize ourselves. It is at times like these that we should not "be afraid to try again". If we don't try how can we ever succeed? If we don't know ourselves how can we do what's best for us? So, once in a while, we should take a chance and get to know "the stranger" within. It'll be good for all of us…

"Carved In Stone" 2013

"A WHITER SHADE OF PALE", PROCOL HARUM, DERAM, 1967

We often don't know what's right there in front of us… No matter what we might want to believe, what we think is out there, or what others tell us the case may be, we can still be uncertain. The words we use to describe it to others may have no meaning if "the truth (isn't) plain to see". Without insight into what we're looking at, it might as well be that our eyes are all "closed". There may be beauty, happiness and opportunity standing right there before us, but how are we to be sure? The world is like a mirage just waiting for us to let ourselves be deceived…many a desert dweller has fallen to the lure of a false oasis. Mountain climbers will tell you that the summit lies just over that next ridge. Deep sea divers have seen creatures with more arms than they could count. Neptune went after a mermaid who took him "for a ride". Though, what we may think of as pleasure can just as easily turn into pain. The cards we hold might not lead us to gain. The words that are meant to be spoken could benefit us better if we were to refrain. "Music (may) be the food of love" and "laughter…its queen", but sometimes, whether we admit it or not, "dirt… is clean". So, if the truth is to be told, we should all be careful what we wish for. If we're not sure of what we want, if we can't see what's right in front of us, and "truth", like reality, slips straight through our fingertips, then we might want to take a moment to contemplate. We have to be open and honest with others and, most importantly, ourselves. Otherwise, without being able to navigate through all the lies, the voyage we're on will have us turning "a whiter shade of pale".

"Unchartered Territory" 1998

Clear a Path to the Future

When the basics are taken care of- the everyday needs, wants, and desires- and the chores are accomplished- the past settled, foundations built, and seeds sown- that is the moment we can start to contemplate what lies ahead... The road before us bears many options, each of which has its own and varied rewards. Yet, not every opportunity is a path down which we should follow. Knowing our own selves will tell us which of those routes we should entertain. Not every venture is to be set out upon by all individuals. In each one of us is a uniqueness that guides our every day in every way. We come to those decisions through a multitude of experiences and a volume full of tales. Most of what we know has been obtained by us first hand. Though, often, we learn just as much from others. With that knowledge combined we have to make sense of what it means. Somehow, we also have to figure out how all of that affects us. Only then will we know what's in the best interest for us. At some point we have to decide where we are going, what we want to do, and who do we want to join us on the journey. So, when we've laid our ground-work, weighed all the alternatives, and gathered our thoughts, we can continue. Taking into account all of those considerations, having removed the obstacles in front of us leaves us with a road that remains a clear path to the future...

"On The Farm" 1976

"WHILE YOU SEE A CHANCE",
STEVE WINWOOD, ISLAND, 1980

Opportunity is the chance for change… Change, as they say, is inevitable. So, if things must change, why don't we do what we can to make things best for us, our family, and our friends? It's easy when we know how. Though, most of us are uncertain of this course. And, the rest of us are unsure of where this will lead us. Change is certain, but we are not…how are we to get the confidence to make the decisions that will be best for us? Is experience, with the risk of making mistakes, the only road to success? Can other's advice, relying on the errors that they've made, lead us to where we need to be? Most of what we have to do is to keep our eyes, ears, and, especially, mind open to the possibilities that are out there for us. When it comes to making the right choices happen, "it's all on (us)." No one is going to look out for our best interests like we would. Everyone else may think they know what we want. Though, most of them would be wrong… Some of them might even tell us how they are actually right, we are definitely wrong, and therefore they know what to do. Instead, we should listen quietly to ourselves and make our move when we're ready to do so, based on our own thoughts. If we don't live life on our own terms, whose life would we be living? Remember, "no one gives (us) anything" that we, our selves haven't already asked for. If we don't know what we need, how can we get what we want? Making our self available to our own thoughts and emotions, especially to love, and to all of life's possibilities is what's in our own best self interest. The only way to be successful in these matters is to think "while (we) see a chance, take it"…

"One More Step" 1999

"DID YOU EVER HAVE TO MAKE UP YOUR MIND?", THE LOVIN' SPOONFUL, KAMA SUTRA, 1965

Choices: the more there are, the harder they are to make…with infinite options, decisions become impossible. Even with finite variables, the process is no less harrowing. "Right and wrong", "yes and no", and "left and right" can be just as tough conclusions to reach. We all know how difficult it is; the ability to be in control is outweighed by the possibility to be criticized. We know what we want, we know what we need, and we know what we desire. Though, we hesitate, and can even put ourselves in a state of momentary paralysis, when we stop to think. And, we all do it… we second-guess ourselves. Or, worse, we second-guess what others would think of what we do. So, if "(we) ever (had) to make up your mind", we know exactly how it feels. A simple thing like "(having) to finally decide" becomes a big chore. Sometimes having one option more than none is mind boggling. Just toggling between the two choices can turn out to be never ending. Wrapping our head around all the ramifications of each choice is overwhelming. We play out all the scenarios that might follow each option. After all is said and done, we've done nothing; therefore, when we come to that point in our life where we can go one way or the other, we should just commit to doing so. Because, if we want to eventually get somewhere, "(we'd) better finally decide"…

"Where To From Here…" 2004

"WITH A LITTLE HELP FROM MY FRIENDS", THE BEATLES (JOE COCKER), A & M RECORDS, 1969

"With a little help from (our) friends" you can do just about anything... Just recall, when we were younger, how building a fort, making a go-cart, going to the beach, or playing a game was almost always done with others. We wouldn't think of doing these things alone, unless we had to, if there was absolutely no one else around. We even associated people with the things we liked to do the most: going to the movies with one friend, bowling with another, talking with a confidant, and maybe hanging out with someone else. Yeah, we all have our "best" friend, or friends, when we're young or times are good. Yet, when times get rough or we get older, we tend to forget about doing things together and relying on others for their help. We want to feel as if we can do it on our own without imposing on anyone else. We don't want to bother them with our troubles. Though, if we thought back to how we got to where we are now, it was always with the help of a friend...we wouldn't think of getting by without "a little help from (our) friends". The only way we were "going to try" was with them. Whether it was to sing, find "somebody to love", or just about anything we did it together. So, now when we need it most, we should remember how we felt when we were "alone" and tried to do things on our "own". Only then will we be reassured that we would do and be better off when someone else is there with us, as we try to get by...

"You Wash My Back..." 2007

"LEAN ON ME",
BILL WITHERS, SUSSEX, 1972

We all need each other…we can't make it on our own. There are some days where it might be OK to be alone. Though, there are other days where it is definitely not alright. Which of those days is it going to be? We can never know: Each and every day starts the same. We get up knowing that there will be good days and bad. There will be times when we are happy and others when we are sad. Though, it's not always foreseeable, and most assuredly not always our fault. No matter how hard we try, things won't always go our way. No matter how much we plan there's always something we haven't thought of. At times like those, we react. And, regrettably, "sometimes in our lives" we have "pain… sorrow… (and we're) not strong". It is times like these that, unfortunately or fortunately, we "need somebody to lean on". Whether it's us on them or them on us, the support should be interchangeable. Because, you see, there'll always be a time where each one of us needs to "carry on… borrow… (or get a) hand". There is nobody that doesn't need somebody sometime. Whether it's for the little things or the big moments in life, we all need to "share (our) load". If we're going to make it we have to be "wise… swallow (our) pride… (and call on) a friend". "We know that there's always tomorrow", yet we have to make it through today. That being the case, short of doing something rash, we need to get past whatever it is that's holding us back… To do so, we have to realize that there are some problems that we can't work out on our own. In those situations we have to search out, be open to, and find someone who understands, so we can "lean on" them.

"Lean On Me" 2002

"HONESTY",
BILLY JOEL, COLUMBIA, 1978

If we're going to make it in this life we have to be honest…there's no *ifs ands* or *buts* about it. This is one of the most profound things we will ever have to consider. And, just as importantly, as we do so, we have to be as honest as possible to ourselves. Just as sincerely, without too much qualification, we have to be honest to others…family, friends and lovers all deserve nothing less than the truth. Yes, we can keep secrets from them, and even, on occasion, from ourselves. Though, the more lies we tell, to them and ourselves, the further we get from who we are. We see that times change and life changes. Though, we often don't see that *we* change. We may tell ourselves that what we are doing is for our, or someone else's, good. Though, we know, whether we want to admit it or not, what is right…right for us, for the moment, and for everyone involved. Doing other than that would only be a lie. We could all lie; it's easy, and may never be caught. Yet, when "(we) look for truthfulness (we) might just as well be blind". That's because, whether we are honest to others or they are honest to us depends on how much we care. The challenge becomes knowing what we're looking for. If we're seeking "tenderness", the truth and "honesty" may be hard to come by. When someone says "they sympathize" they just may be telling us lies when "all (we) want is someone to believe". We may even be able to "find a lover… find a friend… or have security until the bitter end". Though in reality what we really want and need is "sincerity" and someone to "depend on". The difference becomes knowing truth from fiction… In a world where "honesty" can be "such a lonely word" and "hardly ever heard", it can be "mostly what (we) need".

"On The Left Bank" 1976

"THE TIMES THEY ARE A-CHANGIN'", BOB DYLAN, COLUMBIA, 1964

The only certainty we have is uncertainty… The only consistency we have is change… As sure as we are about some things we are just as unsure about others… As positive as we are that things will be different, we know that some things will, for long periods of time, remain the same. It's only to what degree of uncertainty about the things we care about and certainty about the things that don't matter that is of importance. We may say that we, as individuals, as part of the larger group we belong to, as siding with the like-minded thinkers from the four corners of the world, won't change. Though, how can we think or say this when we know all around us, "the times they are a changing"? We see the world around us still spinning, day after day. Theories, ideas, and revelations that are good and bad, right and wrong, strong and weak come and go. It may be that the thoughts, speakers and ones spoken to are different from moment to moment. Yet, we, at all times, have to remain ourselves. When the water starts rising, we have to "start swimming", or we'll "sink like a stone". When the "writers and critics" start prophesying, we have to hope we're not the ones they're "naming". When "senators and congressmen" don't "heed the call", we better hold on while the "battle…is raging". When "mothers and fathers" can't understand their "sons…and daughters" we'll all have to agree to "lend (a) hand". In the end, whether we want to hold onto things or not, what was will no longer be. What is now, for all intents and purposes, will soon be gone. It's not hard to imagine that slow and fast, present and past, and first and last will trade places…if that's the case, then we have to be strong. We have to be sure that we know who we are, who we're with, and where we stand. Otherwise, the winds of change can blow us clear off our foundations. When we're on solid ground with ourselves, then it won't matter what the "times" are.

"This Ship Hasn't Sailed Yet" 2007

"REFUGEE",
TOM PETTY & THE HEARTBREAKERS, BACKSTREET, 1979

Everybody just wants to be free…nobody wants to have on chains that bind them. Sometimes these shackles are real, but often times they are just imagined. What keeps one person down or back is different from what keeps another person from moving ahead. What it takes for each one of us to be released from these ties also depends on the circumstances…what put us in our hold in the first place is what matters. Was it something we did or something we said? Was it *when* we did that something; or where it was done? Or, was it more about the how and why of it? Whatever the reasoning behind our actions, now it's over and done. So, we have to live with our actions and their consequences. Yet, no matter what these occurrences may have been, we "don't have to live like a refugee". Whether "somewhere, somehow, somebody" had whatever, wherever, whenever done to them, or they did it to us, almost doesn't make a difference. Once it's over, and the dust settles, then we have to move on… We're certain, without knowing the details; it's almost always easier said than done. Though, it won't help to worry about what we know or they think. "It don't make no difference" to me, you, or anybody who is within ear shot. What is of our only concern is that we get on with our lives. We have to "fight to be free" of that which keeps us from going forward. Yes, sometimes the walls are real and can't actually be scaled. Whereas, other times the hurdles only appear to be beyond our stride. More often than not, neither extreme is really the case. When that's the situation, what we have to do is take to the highest ground and look in all directions. Then, and only then, will we be able to "see" our way clear to be free.

"The Tide Will Turn" 2008

"YOU CAN'T GET WHAT YOU WANT (TIL YOU KNOW WHAT YOU WANT)", JOE JACKSON, A & M RECORDS, 1984

We all think we know what we want, even though that's often not true...we see what others have, and imagine they know what's best. We think about how we would like to have the same, and that would make us like them. We think about fortune, fame, and power, and all that would get us. We think about love, laughter, and happiness, and how easy that would come then. We think about what we've had in the past, what we have now in the present, and what we'd like in the future- based on their standards. We are sure that's what we want, because it's what everybody else strives for...though, sometimes, if we take the time to think about it, we find it's not what we want at all. That's because, for the most part, we're not listening to ourselves. Our inner voices should guide us, though those words are often drowned out by the mindless chatter of others. Every day we are bombarded with thoughts, images, and ideas, most of which are not our own. What we need to do is to listen for someone who knows what's best for us. This is especially important when we're by ourselves, "feeling... lost and lonely", and "it's all been in (our) mind". Even when we're "reaching out for something" because there'll "always (be) something there". Yet, we "can't see (or hear) that all (we) need is one thing...if it's right". So, what we need to do is take the time to quietly, clearly, and confidently express to ourselves the desires from within. Only then will we be able to put a voice to what is, and will be, fulfilling for both our heart and soul. Only once we've looked inside, and determined what the truth is for us, can we move on. Then, we can eventually figure out how to "get what (we) want". Though, we have to take that first step in the right direction. All the rest will occur naturally...after we "know what (we) want".

"Sunset Under The Palms" 1997

"STAND BY ME",
BEN E. KING, ATCO, 1962

There are many things that come our way in life, good and bad, right and wrong, easy and hard...some are quite benign, meaningless, and painless to deal with. Others need a little more from us than we are willing to admit, able to give, or can handle alone. Though, we're not always sure which of those situations will be the one that's just around the next corner. We never know if it's going to be one of those times where we need someone by our side. As we go through life, we have to be prepared for whatever may come our way. That being said, it's just always better off having someone there with us. No, that doesn't mean we need someone there every single minute of every single day. Yes, it does mean that there should be a person for us there where and when we call. So, when times are good or things go bad, they'll be there. So, when things go right or we've been wronged, they'll be there. So, when life is easy or we find it quite hard, they'll be there. What we need to know in life is that we don't have to "be afraid". And, the only way we can do that is if there's someone ready to "stand" with us. Walking alone in the "dark" is no way to live. Looking at the "sky" and the "mountains" with someone else we "won't shed a tear". We can manage whatever comes our way, "just as long as (they) stand by (us)". We'll know that whenever there's "trouble" we won't have to be on our own. Even when we are by our selves, there'll be someone who we can count on to be there for us when we call. All we want from them is to say yes, when we ask them the question, will you "stand by me"?

"...Way Down There" 2006

"VIENNA",
BILLY JOEL, COLUMBIA, 1977

We all know there's someplace we ought to be…we just want to be there now and forever. Though, we don't often realize that we can't just go anywhere…and that wherever it is won't be the same as we imagined it to be. In our minds, we think that it will be the perfect place and being there will make all the difference, so, if only we were there now all our problems would be solved. Yet, we need to "slow down", because, as they say, getting there is half the fun. What's our "hurry" should be our motto. As we know, there's only "so many hours in the day". If we spend all our time worrying, we won't get what we want we'll "just get old". We don't want to turn around and look back at our life as having not done what we should've, or what we could've. We have to understand that we're "doing fine". We can't be everything to everyone all of the time. Especially, we have to take into consideration that we can't get "ahead" of ourselves. When we do, we "forfeit what we need" by going only after what we want. In doing so, we often lose sight of what's "right" by focusing on what's "wrong". Then we let our "pride" get in the way of our "passion", and, as we know, "only fools are satisfied". So, as we "realize" that we can take our time and look for what we want, we can "disappear for a while". Only then will we be able to pursue our dreams, knowing full well not to "imagine that they'll all come true". Though, whatever happens and wherever it occurs won't be by necessity, but will be by choice…

"Not Quite There…" 1976

"I STILL HAVEN'T FOUND WHAT I'M LOOKING FOR", U2, ISLAND, 1987

Wherever we go, whenever we get there, whatever we know, and however we know it, doesn't mean that all these things add up to help us to solve life's mysteries… When we search for what will make us whole, there may be no clues along the way. We are going to have to seek out and find the answers that will aid our quest on our own. We might have to climb the "highest mountains" and "…run through the fields" to be with the one we believe will know what to do for us. We may not be sure what questions we want answered, or even know how to ask them. Though, we'd certainly "crawl" and "scale…city walls" to be with them and try. We'd look to their advice, or for some sign, some feeling to guide us in the right direction. "Honey lips" or "healing…fingertips" may be what we think we want or need. Yet, those touches may be the furthest thing from what will honestly help. When we're looking for what we want, as we all know, we often times…lose track of what we need. So, no matter what may sound like words that have come from "the tongue of angels", we may actually be holding "the hand of the devil". Be aware that what may seem like paradise is not necessarily so. The only way we can know what is the truth is to go out and look for it. We have to ask the questions and not be afraid of the answers. We have to accept that we may not know everything, and that others can help. Though, we have to realize that if and when our "bonds" of ignorance are broken we shouldn't be ashamed of our newfound knowledge. Until that day, we have to keep on searching, even if we "still haven't found what (we're) looking for".

"A Balcony With A View" 1976

"STAIRWAY TO HEAVEN",
LED ZEPPELIN, ATLANTIC RECORDS, 1971

As we all "know, sometimes words have two meanings"…we're pretty sure that's something we didn't have to be taught. Though, often times we forget about the difference between what is meant and what could be implied. "All that glitters is gold" is a perfect example of that fallacy. Yet, 'all that is gold most assuredly glitters' is an obvious correction. So, how do we know when it's the one thing and not the other? How can we be certain when it's this and not that? Why can't we believe that what we do today will get us what we want tomorrow? When will we know that "all of our thoughts are not misgivings"? When will we stop having doubts that make us "wonder"? What will happen if we continue to let "the piper… lead us to reason"? Won't we have to at some point determine what the truth is for us and which path we should take? Wouldn't it be best if we made a decision and didn't stand around waiting for another to decide our fate? Otherwise, should we be surprised to find out that "the forests…echo with laughter"? If we truly have free will and destiny in our own hands, then why don't we make the most of it? As the song says; "There are two paths (we) can go by, but in the long run there's still time to change the road (we're) on". So, it's never too late to make a course correction or a readjustment of attitude- or altitude, as the case may be. Take the high road, choose the "stairway" that's right and we just might find ourselves on the "whispering wind". In the end, the only things that matter are those choices that make a difference in our life or the lives of people that are important to us. To do so, we must realize that "all are one and one (are) all". Remember, when it comes to living by principles, we must not waver. We have to stand firm, choose what to do, be willing to act on that decision, and only then head in the right direction. "Be a rock and (try) not to roll" is a great motto, upon reflection…

"Ain't No Mountain…" 2006

"TAKE THE LONG WAY HOME",
SUPERTRAMP, A & M RECORDS, 1979

We know that the shortest distance between any two points is a straight line…though the difference between any two ideas may turn out to be immeasurable. What we might believe is right for us may be completely wrong for someone else. What we know as being true by our accounts might be considered false by someone with an opposing view. It may be daytime for half the world, but the rest sleeps, unconcerned. Should everybody be up at the same time, or is it alright to close our eyes once in a while? Can we all be of the same opinion on all matters, or is better that everyone isn't in agreement? More importantly, do we all need to take the same path to get to the same place? The risk lies in some of us missing the stops we need to make, as some unfortunately reach the same destination over and over again. With that being said, sometimes it is better that, on occasion, each one of us has the opportunity to "take the long way home"…in doing so, we get to look at, think about, and experience things in ways we may not have, had we taken the same short cut. With this new perspective we can not only broaden our horizons but also those of others we come in contact with. We no longer will be accused of "never (seeing) what (we) want to see". We'll be looking right at it and at the same time peering at ourselves. Sometimes we have to look outside of our realms to notice the changes within- when times are good, we rarely do so. Most of the time we don't need to adjust our course; though, when our "life's become a catastrophe", if we don't take an alternate route, how will we ever "grow"? Who wants to look back and "see what (we) could've been, what (we) might've been, if (we'd) had more time"? Wouldn't it make more sense to take a moment now, and think about things as we "settle down"? Couldn't we justify not being "around" as having the space to contemplate? Shouldn't we explain that we came to our decision by taking that extra time, as we took "the long way home"?

"There'll Always Be Another…" 1976

"DON'T LET THE SUN GO DOWN ON ME", ELTON JOHN, MCA RECORDS, 1974

Each one of us needs a little light in our life…though it's not so often plain to see. What we regard as illuminating for us; is often times dimming to others. Like the sun, what is bright in our life cannot always be seen directly. Unlike the sun, our lives can cast shadows on places and people we do not choose. We hope to shine our love in a direction where some will find its way back; though, as with many of our best intentions, our feelings are not always reflected back. Our shadows somehow belie and deceive others from what we truly believe. Sometimes we "can't light…more of (our) darkness". And then we have to "save (ourselves) from falling". We don't want to "let the sun go down on (us)". Without that light, there is no other source of brightness. With only darkness, there is no way that anyone else can see. We need to bring the truth out into the open, for all to gaze upon. It's too easy for meanings to be "misread", when not seen in the right hues. Like a plant needs only certain wavelengths of sunlight to grow, does love, too, need to be shone upon it in just the right way to thrive? We shouldn't hide our feelings, misrepresent our emotions, or complicate our thoughts. Each of these things only goes to lengthen the shadow cast between one another. Only when all is clear, uncovered, and lit up can we see each other as we are. To see things as they are is to believe, to believe things as they may be is to love, and to love without changing a thing…can only happen if we keep the light shining.

"There It Goes…" 1984

"IF YOU LOVE SOMEBODY SET THEM FREE", STING, A & M RECORDS, 1985

As much as we want to hold near and dear everything we love, we just can't do it…besides being physically impossible, it's emotionally draining. Imagine the time and effort it would take to sort through and arrange all of our connections and things. Realize what it would mean in terms of time to do this on a constant basis. Who would have the energy to make readjustments when someone or something new came into their life? Are there more important uses of our resources than that? What do we keep and can we throw anything away? What will people think if we let something go? How do we survive without having everything we need at all times? Will we be the same person if we don't have the things that made us who we are? Is there any way we can go on empty handed? The answer is absolutely, yes. Intuitively, we already knew this. Intellectually, we can rationalize any argument for or against any of our decisions. Though, when it comes to our insecurities, we feel the need to hold onto everything we ever thought had any meaning or power in our life. The unfortunate thing is that it may take us a lifetime to find out it's just the opposite. Keeping "something precious" doesn't mean locking "it up" and throwing "away the key". It means appreciating it and respecting it, even if that entails never having rights to or owning it. The "it" that we're talking about doesn't really matter. Things are just that and we can always get by with less or different. Necessities, on the other hand, are by definition essential. The air, water, food, clothing, and shelter available to us can affect the quality and quantity of our lives. Yet, only love truly makes a difference in either. With love being so vital to our existence, it's a wonder why we don't know how to handle it better than we do. Treating the people we love like a "possession" will either make them feel like their suffocating or force them to want to leave. Only by giving them the choice of what to do will we know where they really want to be? So, to answer the question of whether they will stay or go, we have to consider "if (we) love somebody, set them free"…

"Flight Of Fancy" 2008

"TEACH YOUR CHILDREN",
CROSBY, STILL, NASH & YOUNG, ATLANTIC RECORDS, 1970

It seems the more we learn, the less we know… the older we get, the younger we want to be. We'll never understand why mistakes are only allowed in our youth. It doesn't make sense why we can't keep on trying new things as we age. We're born with curiosity and should carry that with us wherever we go. We live our lives with questions that need answers. Does it matter where our answers- or for that matter, our questions- come from? Can't we seek knowledge from any source that advocates truth, reason, and rationality? We're taught from an early age that goodness, fairness and justice are part of "a code that (we) can live by". We live each day searching for guidance, advice, and wisdom to get us through. We grow up wanting to become respected, trusted, and loved as we pursue our "dreams". It's surprising how we don't see that it's all right there in front of us. How we keep passing by one opportunity after another is amazing. We all have what it takes to get us through the day. We all were given everything we ever needed to be successful. Inherent in our being is the ability to learn. Required for our survival is the necessity to teach. Without the one we could not have the other. From generation to generation, parents have been passing down more than just their genes. Children, for their part, have been taking what they could to "become" who they'll be. What both groups don't understand is that in doing so they are helping each other. Too often, this nuance is what's lost in transition. The ability to give and take and return the favor will "slowly go by". So, when they offer their time to us, we should listen. That goes for parents talking to children and vice-versa. Only in retrospect can we appreciate how important this is, and that "the past is just a good bye". Therefore, we should hear every word they say and "don't ever ask them why", just…"know they love you".

"Gone Fishing" 1996

"YOU CAN'T ALWAYS GET WHAT YOU WANT", THE ROLLING STONES (M. JAGGER/K. RICHARDS), DECCA, 1969

Maybe one of the best known anthems in all of rock "n" roll lore is: "You can't always get what you want, but if you try sometimes you just might find that you get what you need"…how much truer and simpler can it get? What more can be said on the matter of accepting what is? Though in saying those words, it often doesn't seem to be, or have to be, that way. What if you stop wanting things in the first place? Maybe you'll get what you need without asking for it? It's a hard concept to follow, let alone to live by. Who doesn't want things? Where would we all be if we only lived to get what we need? Is there any way that we would all be better off if we could have a balance between the two? Of course! The trick lies in knowing what's important to each one of us…understanding our hopes, dreams, and desires is of utmost priority. Accepting our needs, wants, and when to compromise between the two is crucial. Usually, when we're willing to give up one thing we're more likely to get something else in its place. Oftentimes, when we do have to make sacrifices, we're more apt to appreciate what we have. Having choices is good, but making decisions is better. Knowing what's right for us, even if it's only right for now, is paramount. Not wasting so much time and energy on things we can't have or shouldn't go after in the first place will be beneficial. Being unchained must-haves and got-to-dos allows us to focus on what really matters in our life. Living without destinations and distractions has so many advantages. When we go about our days and nights as though they were the only ones we had, we're always more determined. We get so much done, have a hard time seeing the negative, and get along so well with others. Life will never be perfect, but if we can make it that much easier why don't we? We "just might find that (we) get what (we) need"…

"The Challenge" 1984

"RUNNING ON EMPTY",
JACKSON BROWNE, ASYLUM, 1977

In this life we have to keep moving forward...we know that we must to survive. Like a shark, we might die if we stop. So we take it one day, one step, and one thought at a time. If we tried any other way, that could kill us too. It's so hard to think ahead, and it's just as hard to think behind. Though, why is it ever so much more difficult to think about the moment? One day we were seventeen, the next twenty-one, and now look at us. How could it be? What did we know then, when did we learn it, and why won't it help us now? Could it be that we just have to keep "running"? Is it to "keep (our) love alive"? Would it be easy to confuse it "with what (we) do to survive"? Or, is it that we "need some reason to believe"? Every which way life's draining us and it feels like we're "running on empty". Day turns into night, night turns into day, and the road turns from one into another. We don't know or remember how we got on this one. Yet, does it really matter? Here we are, running "empty", "blind", "into the sun", and "behind". However, for whatever reason, and no matter how, we keep going. There must be something to it, to us, or to both things. The road may be long, it may be narrow, it may have potholes and it may take its toll on or from us. Whatever the case, it's our road and we're not going to give up on it. We're going to see what it has in store for us, not knowing what we'll find, and remembering to forget to look at the gas gauge...without filling up, we take the chance, because we just have to keep going even while "running on empty".

"Where Will It End..." 2007

"AND WHEN I DIE",
BLOOD, SWEAT & TEARS, COLUMBIA, 1968

And, when we live…"Give (us our) freedom"! How much more basic a plan can one have than that? That request is made knowingly that someday we'll all be gone. Though, having the knowledge of where, when, or maybe how that will be eludes most of us. We are certain of one thing: that having been born, the moment of truth is inescapable for us. Yet, we are grateful for all that life has to offer us in between… even the opportunity to contemplate our time here, or reason for being. Our parents made that chance a reality, and, ultimately, our destiny. With a bit of luck, timing, and the right circumstances, maybe we can return the favor to the universe. "One child born in this world to carry on" would be an honorable motto to follow. Who else could or would keep our thoughts alive when we're "gone"? Yes, not everyone is so fortunate enough to have progeny. Or, for that matter, not everyone should, could, or may even choose to have offspring. Yet, all will be well, never-the-less, if each of us has at least one person to take up our case, and eventually our place…to fight the good fight, we live our lives "not scared of dying" and ask only "to have no chains on (us)". We are aware that there are natural, man-made, and other ways that may hold us back as we try to move forward with our lives. Somehow, we keep going anyway, knowing full well, that no one, including us, has any idea what is in store for them. Each and every one of us tries to live as healthy, happy, and free a life, devoid of as many negative influences as possible. No matter what our course, cause, motive, or inclination is we aim to be unaffected. We go about our days and nights, as one amongst so many others, knowing it is not an easy task. We take each day on its own, for what it is, and hope for the best. So, when it comes time to claim we're ready, please let us just "go naturally"…

"He's The Man" 1976

Keep Your Dreams Alive

For it all to work there remains one last chore…as important as the first step is in any journey, so is the follow-through, leading us to wherever Life will take us. That means taking everything we know, reflecting on everything we've done, and having the confidence that we can complete what was started. It doesn't matter if it's climbing mountains, winning awards, or just making a new friend. What is important is that our goal is something that is a want, need, desire- or a dream- that will keep us going. We all have to have that one thing that makes us get up in the morning, work our way through the day, and lets us put our head down at night knowing what we're doing matters. Even if we're not succeeding at the moment, have been distracted for an extended time, or lost our way the time being…we still will have our dreams. The quest is to find and grab hold of that wish, look at it carefully from all sides, and let it go into the air- to see which way it takes us. For, to follow that course, we may find ourselves in unchartered territory, be afraid along the way, or head down roads we never could've imagined. Though, without our pursuit there would only be doubt, regret, and disillusionment. How can we live our lives wondering what if? Why should we imagine what should've been? When will we take the bull by the horns and ride? The answer to all those questions can be found in the actions we take every single day. If we make every possible effort to know who we are, take every potential opportunity to become who we're supposed to be, and remember why we're doing it all along the way; then and only then will we be able to keep our dreams alive…

"Life Is A Journey…" 2007

"AQUARIUS/LET THE SUN SHINE IN",
THE 5ᵀᴴ DIMENSION, DUNHILL, 1969

Astrology, psychology, mythology, and the study of every other force in the universe can only help us if we let it…letting it means understanding it. Which is to say, accepting its strengths and weaknesses, and how each of those things affects us. What we have to realize is that everything around us matters. All that was, is, and will be are connected. What's set into motion often has a will of its own. To change this outcome someone has to put in significant effort. The action of that *someone* often guides the reactions of others. When all is said and done, only then might there be "harmony and understanding, sympathy and trust abounding". To reach that point each one of us has to trust and respect ourselves, and, of course, others. That means freedom from "falsehoods or derisions", inflicted by self or non-self. It also includes "living dreams of visions", where what's imagined is possible…it would be a place where we could reveal our inner-most thoughts. That would be "the mind's true liberation". Then we could lead our lives guided by "peace" and steered by the "stars", whatever we chose those things to mean. For each one of us believes in what we want to believe in, and that's more than alright- that's just. In the end, what really matters is being open and honest to everyone, and, most importantly, to our selves. In doing so, we give everyone, including ourselves, the opportunity to know who we really are. Once we know each other we can let everyone be who they were meant to be. Letting each and every one of us be ourselves only adds to an equally shared world view. If everyone sees that we all have the right to be here and do what we're doing, then love will "let the sun shine in" on us all…

"Reaching For The Light" 2012

"IMAGINE",
JOHN LENNON, APPLE, 1971

We all have dreams…some of us want fame and fortune, others want influence and power, and the rest want something altogether different. That difference may be for themselves or others, for some and not others, or for one and all. When there's something that is going to affect all, including ourselves, we tend to listen. We may like it or not, have an opinion about it or not, want to change it or just leave it alone. But, we all want to know how we're going to have to respond. Will we have to do a lot, will we have to do a little, or won't we have to do anything at all? In a world where everything is perfect, there's nothing that needs to be done. When things are good enough, maybe only minor adjustments need to be made. Yet, when no one can agree and everyone is out for themselves, there's quite a bit to do. And, that starts with each one of us…we have to "imagine" what the possibilities are. We need to live "for today" and "in peace". We want to be able to see the potential where "the world will be as one". Only then can we reflect on "all the people sharing all the world". Since we each have the right to be here, we also have the responsibility to do our part. That means taking the opportunity for ourselves and allowing everyone else along the way to dream. That means being accountable for our actions- and getting our jobs done, as well. We still have to live each and every day, with ourselves and with each and every other person in our life. Though, when we all pull together and work for the same goals, at the end of the day everyone can "join" one another and follow our dreams…"Imagine".

"Is It Really There…" 2004

"BLOWIN' IN THE WIND",
BOB DYLAN, COLUMBIA, 1963

When we listen carefully enough, we can hear… When we look clearly enough, we can see… When we speak directly from the heart, will anyone listen? It takes some, more than others, a while to hear…yet, can we blame them? We, ourselves, often take time to let words sink in. How many voices have spoken to us that we have not heard? How many suggestions have been given to us that we let fall by the wayside? How many ideas were shared with us that we didn't help carry through? The answers, as the song says, are "blowin' in the wind". We don't have to "walk down" any more roads, or have "white doves sail" any more seas, and fly any more "cannon balls" to find these…everything we need to know is available to each and every one of us, each and every day. We don't need to "look up", or have "many ears", and have "many deaths" occur to be sure of this. Each and every one of us has the luxury of having had many others come before them. So, we don't have to wait for any mountains to be "washed to the sea", or for all people to be "allowed to be free", and for others to turn their heads "pretending (not to) see". Each and every one of us has the opportunity to take all the knowledge, use all the wisdom, and look at all the mistakes that have been made before…right now. We can combine all of our talents and abilities to do what is necessary to make our world a place where everyone can follow what is best for them. In allowing this, at the same time, we also make it easier for ourselves. Could there be anything better than that, for us or for them? The answer, we know, is…

"The Road To…" 2004

"DREAM WEAVER",
GARY WRIGHT, WARNER BROTHERS RECORDS, 1975

If only there was someone who could guide our dreams…someone to take us by the hand and walk us through all of life's ups and downs, someone who would congratulate us when we did well and console us when we didn't, and someone to explain to us, without judging, where we did right and when we did wrong. The person who could help us in these ways- and maybe some others- would be irreplaceable. The ability to have a better life would be invaluable. To close your eyes at night and not be afraid would be incredible. Though, we shouldn't dream our lives away…dreams are a means to an end. To dream is to imagine the impossible. To dream is to have faith that there are answers to your questions. To dream is to be able to enunciate what you could not otherwise put into words. To dream is to be human… to be human is to have "worries of today" and want to "get through the night". To be human is to "reach the morning light" and be able to "forget today's pains". To be human is to live, make mistakes, and to move on. So, really what each of us needs is someone to take assessment of who we are, where we've gone, and what we've done. In making this judgment they must be fair, reasonable, and take all factors into consideration. The analysis must be concise, unbiased, and constructive. The person who puts all of this together must mesh what was, what is, and what will be into one. They must draw from the fabric and texture that makes up our lives. The cloth that results must cover us and protect us from all of life's storms. There's no one who knows us better, can spin those threads more exactly, and would lead us in the direction we need to be going- than us. We could, would, and should be our own "dream weaver"…

"Into The Night…" 1996

"COLOUR MY WORLD",
CHICAGO, COLUMBIA, 1970

Everybody dreams…many say their visions are in color. A few say the images are in black and white. Some people remember every detail of what occurred while they slept. Others wake not recalling even a feeling about what transpired the night before. A handful of people arise changed and ready to act upon their insights. Most would say that they don't even understand what their dreams mean. Though, almost everybody would agree that it's important to have dreams… Whether it's the kind at night, or the ones where we drift off during the day, or the plans we have for the future- they all matter. To dream is to hope. To hope is to imagine change. To imagine change is to see possibilities. Possibilities are what we all live for. The possibility to have it better than we do now, to be with that someone we want in the future, or to be free of the things that are holding us back. Those are all the things we really ever ask for… A life with potential is like a dream unbound. Who could ask for anything more? To be able to get up in the morning and head off to where we want, with whom we want, and to do what we want is a dream… Knowing that these things are more than just imaginable is without equal. Realizing what was once only a glimmer of hope can be obtainable is quite inspiring. Living a life that is full of meaning, substance, and satisfaction is what we all would like to think of and aspire to. The "promise" of all of this is only made through the possibility of "dreams", which then can fill our "world with hope"…

"Chasing Waterfalls" 1982

"HOUSE AT POOH CORNER",
LOGGINS & MESSINA, LIBERTY, 1970

We all remember back to a time when we felt safe, didn't have a care in the world, and had very few questions go unanswered... When we reflect on that time, we recall the world revolved around us and we liked it. We were happy to go about our day asking for only what we wanted, needed, or had to have in the moment. We knew that everything would be taken care of and that all things would work out in the end. "Posing our questions", we never thought that they could go answered. Or, when answered, we never imagined that what was said wouldn't make sense. Our universe was ordered and free of chaos. One thing led to the other, and nothing would be out of the ordinary. The only one to be "surprised" was when we told someone else something new. We were the explorers, discoverers, and reporters all wrapped into one. There was nothing happening in the world that we weren't a part of. We thought our sphere of influence boundless. The limits of our existence were set only by us. When we needed someone it was only for as long as it took for them to explain something to us, or help us to figure something out and then do whatever it was, by ourselves. Once accomplished, we moved on to bigger and better things. The more complicated the task, meaningful the result, or import for to our future, the greater our assessment of what we did. These events, and the objects which we associate with them, are the "precious things" that meant the most to us. "Throughout all our lives, after all's said and done" these things still have power. No matter how long it has been, what we have gone through, and where else we have been, they still hold the same meaning for us. These things take us back to that place where we felt safe, carefree, and had no unanswered questions. Every once in a while, when the moment's right and we need it the most, we all want to go "back to (those) days…and ways".

"Room With A View" 1978

"DO YOU BELIEVE IN MAGIC?",
THE LOVIN' SPOONFUL, KAMA SUTRA, 1965

There are some things that just move us…sometimes it's a thought, other times it's a vision, at times it's a smell, or even a sound. Music can be one of those things that take us places we've already been, places we'd like to someday be, and places we've never even imagined. And, "if (we) believe in magic" we're almost half way there. "Just go and listen" to the music and we've gone practically the rest of the way. Rock and roll can get us almost anywhere we want to, need to or have to go. Though, we've got to believe to get us all the way there. The spirit may move us, yet, our soul has got to take us. Dreams can only come true if we let them… Dreams can only come true if we dream them… Dreams can only come true if we wake from them… So, let's talk all we can about what can "set (us) free". So, let's go out every chance we get to go dancing "late at night". So, let's go to bed afterwards tired, satisfied, and imagine we're in "an old-time movie". Just remember, whatever we're going to do, we always have to keep an open mind to all of life's possibilities. Opportunities can only happen when we let them. Our senses can only guide us when we're aware of them. Dreams can only come true if we believe in them. Because if we believe, then everyone can believe…and, when we all believe, anything and everything is possible, even "magic".

"If Still Waters Run Deep…" 1998

"FIRE AND RAIN",
JAMES TAYLOR, WARNER BROTHERS RECORDS, 1970

Of all the places, of all the people, and of all the circumstances any one of us have ever come across… we know that there's at least that one moment in time we wish we could have back again. That moment most likely had nothing to do with the timing. That moment most likely wasn't anybody's fault. And, that moment most likely would've occurred one way or the other. Yet, we can't really blame the world on the outcome. Though, sometimes we dream about it and wish we had it to do all over one more time. We play the scene over and over in our head. We think about all the things that have happened since then. We think about all the things that might have happened instead. We may have thought we've seen just about everything, including "fire and rain". Yet, we may have thought nothing of those things at the time. We might have even been lucky enough to live and enjoy some "sunny days that…would never end". Or, we might've lived through "lonely times" where no matter how hard we tried; we "could not find a friend". Though, to this day, we continue to dream. The locations have changed, the faces may be unfamiliar, and we're not the same person we were. So, why is it that we "always thought that (we'd) see (that person) again"? Is it because that person and us, at that time, and in that place, *were* the dream? Was it that at that moment we really had it all? Could it be that if things had worked out differently we would still be living the fantasy? Since it didn't work out that way, isn't life still worth living the way it is now? Is it possible that seeing that person "one more time" would make all the difference in our world? Or, is it, more likely, that letting that person go that day was part of the dream? The truth is this…there's no going back in time, there's no replaying of life's scenes, and there's no changing what happened that day. Therefore, if we keep our hopes up that we'll see that person again and pick up where we left off; we're actually letting our dream die. So, to keep our dream alive, we have to let go…even if it means not seeing them again.

"Above Or Below" 2011

"DRIFT AWAY",
DOBIE GRAY, DECCA, 1973

There are some days that we just can't get anything going... We lie in bed, sit in a chair, or just walk around not knowing what to do next. Somehow, we've lost sight of what our dreams are, or where we're headed, or what needs to be done at the moment to get us there. We either believe there's nothing we can do, or there's no one there to motivate us, or there are too many things happening at once. Either which way, we don't know what option is best. Our tendency is to want to drown out everything. Though, even if we do so, the lack of any sound at all, even in our own mind, winds up being just as disturbing. At times like these, the silence can be even more overwhelming. So, we search our mind, peruse our line of sight, and dig deep within ourselves for something to get us headed in the right direction... If we try with all our might for that motivation, sometimes we give up just a little bit, and in that moment we start to "drift away". Without knowing it, we've let our emotions "carry (us) through". The feelings, the thoughts, the "rhythm and rhyme and harmony" that has always been inside of us takes hold and guides us. For some it's actually music that moves them. For others its beauty that inspires them. For the rest, it could be anything that gets them lost enough that they wind up finding their way. Whatever it is, everyone has or needs something that they can hang onto that allows them to be able to "free (their) soul". At the instant our "mind is free", our body, our heart, and our spirit follow along. No longer are we confused, hesitant, or uncertain about what we should do next. The waves of our thoughts, emotions, and soul will take us to the right course. Then and only then, will we know, be able to, and go where our dreams take us as we "drift away"...

"Without A Worry..." 1996

"LONELY PEOPLE",
AMERICA, WARNER BROTHERS RECORDS, 1974

"You never know until you try" is a motto that we all can live by…whether we're living our dreams or dreaming to live, these words are wise. Whether we've found what we were looking for or are still searching for it, we can't argue with the sentiment. Whether we know what we want or want to know what we can have, there's only one way to find out. So, we should never think "that life has passed (us) by". If it's not too late, and we still have a chance, why don't we take it? If we haven't reached the journey's end, why don't we make the most of it? If we think that we're "lonely", well…everybody's lonely sometimes. We just have to remember that we always have ourselves… Me, myself, and I can be- and often is- enough. We're born into this world alone and we go out of it all on our own. Though, in between we don't ever have to be completely alone. Yes, it's not right that it does occur, and it happens to all of us at some time, but it doesn't have to last forever. So, we never know what life has in store for any of us. We may think we know where we're going, who we're going to see, and what we're going to do. Though, oftentimes someone, something, or a combination of people and things has different plans for us. Life has so many twists and turns that no one can predict even the most obvious of outcomes. Yet, that's what makes it so interesting…around each corner is a new opportunity, and with that comes new possibilities. Chances and risks abound equally. We may think that we've been there, done that, and we don't need to bother. Though, we'd be wrong; it's the bothering that actually matters. How else would our dreams, wants, or desires ever come true? If we don't put in the effort nobody else will do it for us. How do we know this? Anyone who's ever bothered to try can tell us so. Therefore, we'd better bother to do what we need to do, because nobody else will bother for us or with us unless we try…

"Through The Mist" 1999

"THE PRETENDER",
JACKSON BROWNE, ASYLUM, 1976

We all start out as "the pretender" and hope we are never the one that has to "surrender"... From the moment we are born until the day we die, we search for what makes us who we are. No matter what life has to offer, we learn that it is full of choices and "changes". We go on to realize that we're often "caught between" our "longing" and our "struggle". Little did we know that in each decision we make, each new direction we take, and each opportunity we forsake "that all (our) hopes and dreams begin and end there". If only we had known then what we know now, then we wouldn't have any regrets for what we said or did. If only we could go back in time and undo some of the ties that bind us to who we are at the moment. If only we recognized at that time that life was going to turn, and that we had the ability to redirect it. Then, maybe our "paint-by-number dreams" would've looked differently than they do today. Yet, if we think about it, we did make some good decisions along the way. For all its worth, we made choices based on what we knew and what we thought at the time...how else could we have done things otherwise? So, whether we believe rightfully or not, we can still consider ourselves to be "contenders". We still have so many opportunities, directions, and decisions to deal with for and in our future. The only thing we have to remember is that with each of these choices comes the chance to be true to ourselves. No matter how far we may have strayed off course, we can guide ourselves right back to where and who we were meant to be. No longer would we have to pretend to be alright with the way things are. No more would we have to pretend to be someone other than ourselves. Never again would we back down from the fight, to protect our hopes and dreams from "(sailing) out of sight". From now on, until the end, we won't have to...

"Mighty As An Oak" 1998

"PEOPLE GOT TO BE FREE", THE RASCALS, ATLANTIC RECORDS, 1968

Nowhere and never in the history of time and place was there ever a consensus of thought. It mattered more what was being asked, how it was being asked, and what the expected answer was to be. Until, of course, the notion of "people (having the right) to be free". We may say that there are still some places and people that don't believe in this. Though, it's not because they think that it's wrong. It's not that, because it's right. It's just that they don't accept it, where they are and for whatever reason. Accepting and believing are obviously two different things. Yet, even where this is common practice you see that "people…just want to be free". The question then asked should be, "why can't you and me learn to love one another?" It's such a simple question, with such a simple answer, and yet has still so many people finding it hard to contemplate even asking the question. Whether from "deep in the valley… (to) the mountain on out to the sea" most people find freedom reasonable, and maybe even rightful. Whether you agree, or agree to disagree, on the means and the methods of freedom, you'd have to be unreasonable to withhold it from anyone. "*Life, liberty and the pursuit of happiness*" may be one way to say it. "*Live and let live*" is another way. Though, however it is said, by whomever and wherever, it still has the same meaning. People should be able to live, love, laugh, dream, cry, work and do just about anything else they want, within reason. Once again *reason* being the guideline for the freedom all people could have, from which all actions and reactions originate. What a wonderful world we'd have if only everyone agreed to and understood this. If everyone lived their life, didn't interfere with anyone else's life, and maybe even helped one another… that is "the way it should be".

"Out My Window…" 1976

"FREE BIRD",
LYNRYD SKYNYRD, MCA RECORDS, 1973

We shouldn't do those things that will keep us from doing what we want…we shouldn't think about other things that will keep us from what we need. We shouldn't say any words that someday will keep us from finding our dreams. We all have desires, and kind of, sort of, somehow know what it will take to get us there. Sometimes it's a simple matter, no big deal, and we can do it on our own. Other times it's a lot more complicated, quite intricate, and we need someone to help us. Either which way, we have to realize, at least, who we are and how we are in this world… too many people are uncertain about where they fit in the grand scheme of things. Too few people take the time to even consider the big picture. Though, most everyone knows whether or not they have, will make, or can take advantage of a choice in their life. Choosing one thing over another, going one place as compared to the other, and being with one person versus any other is the true day-to-day reality. Yet, how many of us take the time to even consider where these choices leave us. If we were "free as a bird" to look down on our situation, it would be so easy to see where we were. If we knew that "things just couldn't be the same", we'd make our decisions to assure they weren't. If we were sure that we "cannot change", then we would be certain to stay the course and do the best that we can with what we're given. When we're free to be ourselves…everyone may be at fault, but there's no one to blame. Each and every one of us has to lead our own life, and no one can take that away from us. If we're honest to everyone, especially ourselves, then no one, including us, will ever get hurt. Freedom from the pain which comes from not telling the truth is a lofty goal. Soaring above the lies, where the wind of deceit is against us, will always get us farther still. So, if we ever want to reach our dreams, sometimes we have to let go of what's holding us back, and then take off to the sky…

"Proud As A…" 1999

"FLY LIKE AN EAGLE", THE STEVE MILLER BAND, CAPITOL, 1976

Sometimes we realize that we're not the only ones with dreams…sometimes we see that others have dreams of their own. Sometimes we think that everyone can have the same dream. Sometimes we imagine that we can make time stand still. Sometimes we feel that everyone should stop and listen. Sometimes we believe that everyone could believe as we do… Then there are times that we know that's not the way it is, should be, or will ever be. Though, we know we have to do something. We know that no matter what happens, we have to be above it all. We know that doing nothing is not an option, for us. It is times like these, when we all need to go ahead and slip "into the future". It is moments like those that we need to see that we can make a difference. It is only when we get involved that we get to feel any and all connections…we may want to "fly like an eagle", but we can only do so when we're free. We may say "let (our) spirit carry (us)", though we can only do so if we're not weighed down. We may try to make it "through the revolution", yet we can only do so if somehow we've figured out that "there's a solution". We all know the answer lies in the ability for everybody to see as one another does… To see that there's no future unless everyone is included, is quite clear. To think that some of us deserve more, or have rights that others don't, is quite unclear. To imagine that the world could go on as it does, without any changes or consequences, is vague. If we can see to it that everyone believes these things, to see the world as others do, is the only way we might have a chance. If we could take every moment as if it was the only one we had, and an opportunity for others too, then we might make it. If we dare to dream that everyone could be free, then we might realize it. Maybe someday we'll all be able to "fly like an eagle"…

"Above Us There's Only…" 2011

"PEACE TRAIN",
CAT STEVENS, A & M RECORDS, 1971

There's only one way we can take this journey called life, and that's moving forward… No matter how we want to go back a stop or two or jump ahead a few, we're always only at the station called the present moment. In the past we may have done some things, or had things done to us, that we regret, or would like to do over. In the future we may look ahead to better times for us and better actions by others, for a needed change. Yet, it's only in the today, the here and now, this present moment that life really happens. So, no matter how much we think "about the good things to come". And, no matter how much we believe that "something good has begun". It's only a dream come true if we all live in this "world as one"… Now, as we all know, that's easier said than done. And, history has shown that this "peace train" has been slow to come, having been derailed more than a time or two. Though, if we don't want to live our lives forever "on the edge of darkness", we are better off if we all start "sounding louder". If we don't start speaking up and make ourselves heard, then the silence will speak for itself. We can't know about what everybody else is thinking, unless we all think out loud and have our opinions spoken. There's nothing worse than having our decisions made based upon indecision of our own. When we don't speak our mind, we're making no choice for ourselves, which is a choice all the same. So, unless we don't mind, it does matter and we need to speak up. We need to let the world know exactly how we feel. So, when we're ready to board that train, we can go together. One after the other, we can join another and another. And, once we get going, maybe there'll be even more who hear the train coming. And, maybe they'll "bring (their) good friends too". And, if we can get enough people to ride together, maybe we'll all be able to live the same dream. And, once living that way, maybe then we can go "home again" riding that "peace train"…

"Where Do We Go From Here" 1983

"UNITED WE STAND",
BROTHERHOOD OF MAN, TONY MILLER & PETER SIMONS, DERAM, 1970

Wherever we go, whatever we do, why is it that we do it together? Together, forever, we will be to the end from the very start… Some say how, some say why, and we say there is no reason to ever question it. When you mention the two of us, it's always in one breath. When you look at the two of us, it's always in one field of vision. When you think of the two of us it's always with one thought in mind…why isn't it that everyone is with someone else? We know that the fact of the matter has been, is, and will always be, that "united we stand" and "divided we fall". So, why is it that, in this day and age, with all that is known, there are so many people who are still alone? How is it that, with communication so readily available, and languages so easily translatable, that more people don't think the same way? Don't we all want someone there "if our backs should ever be against the wall"? The answer, for us individually or collectively, of course, is an unequivocal *yes*. The reality, we realize, from the history we know, is that it's not always possible. The dream is, without question, that somehow everyone has this experience, at sometime in their life, and gets to know the feeling…the feeling that everyone should have at some point in their life, that *this is how it is meant to be*. The feeling that everyone could have for every point in their life, is that "if the world about (us) falls apart" we know our love will "still be here". The feeling that "if the going gets too hard", when we call our love we know they'll "hear". So, let's keep ourselves open to the sound of all the voices, not only ours, but also theirs. When words are spoken, they have more meaning when there's someone there to hear and respond to them. When we speak, we listen for someone who will answer. When they answer, hopefully we too will hear…that "divided we fall" but "united we stand".

"Ice As Land" 2007

"WHAT THE WORLD NEEDS NOW IS LOVE", JACKIE DESHANNON, IMPERIAL RECORDS, 1965

Just as there is nothing new under the sun, there are some things that, no matter how much we want them to, never change... Just as without the sun there'd be no energy for life, life would not be worth living, no matter what we think, without the energy of love. Love is the bond that keeps everything and everyone, including us, together. Without love, everyone we know and everything we believe in would fly apart. Just like the sun keeps the solar system together, without the gravity of love, we'd all be lost in space. The space we're talking about isn't what's beyond our planet. The space we mean is what will be between us. It won't be "mountains" or "hillsides" and "oceans" or "rivers", but something far worse. Being apart, when we're actually not, is a much greater tragedy. Being separate, when we can be together, is not what is needed. What is needed is something much greater, "that there's just too little of". There are plenty of "cornfields" and "wheat fields" or "sunbeams" and "moonbeams". Though, what we could use a lot more of is "not just for some but for everyone". That, of course, without a doubt, is love. Love brightens up each and every day. Love keeps things from unraveling and spinning out of control. Love is the thing that gets us up in the morning. Love is the last thing we want to think about at night. Who would want to, or even try to, go without it if they could have it? So, if we haven't figured out by now what was missing in the past or what might be needed in the future...then, for sure, we have to realize that "what the world needs now is love".

"The Butterfly Effect" 2006

"GET TOGETHER", THE YOUNGBLOODS, RCA RECORDS, 1967

The here, the now, the moment, and this instant are all one in the same… The past, the present, the future, and all of eternity are not at all the same. What makes one different from another is not just a matter of time. Time is what we make of it…and it is all just "relative". How we relate to this is just as important as what meaning we put into it. If we take for granted the opportunities in front of us, then we probably also don't care about others. If no one or nothing else matters then we probably often wonder and "may not know why". The answer is simple; when the truth is told, "love is but a song to sing". Love is when we don't fear "the way we die". Love is in the knowing that "we shall surely pass". If we can go on even with this knowledge, then it sure sounds as if it would be beautiful… When we don't worry about the things we can't control, we're free to enjoy all that is around us. Beauty is then not only in the eye of the beholder, but also in the voices that the person hears, and the feelings that the person has. So, if responding to our senses is "the key to love and fear", then shouldn't we all keep in constant touch? If that's the solution, how easy would it be for us to unlock the secret of time upon our "command"? Everybody knows what wise men have been saying for ever, that *time doesn't stand still* and *time waits for no man*. Then, if only we would "come on" and "smile" upon and "get together" with "one another", why don't we do it? What do we have to lose, if we listened to what was inside each of us, and allowed ourselves the opportunity to see if it's true? We could then experience all the beauty that this world has to offer us. We could share love, between each of us, and amongst all of us, and make it happen "right now"…

"A View From Afar" 2006

"MIRACLES",
JEFFERSON STARSHIP, RCA RECORDS, 1975

If we were to think upon, imagine, or believe in something, what would it be? Would we put time and energy into something that was impossible, improbable, or highly unlikely? Or, would we put every effort into something that was more than likely, had a good chance, or was never in doubt? If someone felt about us so strongly that they were willing to "move heaven and earth", would that "prove it to (us)"? If someone were to ask us to have "a little faith" and to "know (that) love is the answer", would that sway us? What would, of all the eventualities, occurrences, or emotions we could experience, get us to "feel like swirling and dancing"? Was there ever a time when we felt "it's like having every dream (we) wanted to come true"? Well, for some people it's when they're with the one they love…so strong is the feeling that they'd be willing to do just about anything for it. So powerful is the bond that they'd risk everything from having it fall apart. There are few things in this life that most people would agree upon. Though, love is one of the few exceptions to that rule… When we talk about love, everybody's version of it may be different, but their passion for it is about the same. When we think about love, our definition of it may not fit anyone else's, but we'd both know it if we saw it. When there is love, all of us and all of them would recognize it. So, "if only (we'd) believe…believe in miracles", then we'd be a part of that miracle. And, of course, we would all agree, that miracle is love…

"Just Like That" 2011

"THE LOGICAL SONG",
SUPERTRAMP, A & M RECORDS, 1979

If only we knew, way back when, what we know now…if only we were, so long ago, what we are now… if only we could go back and remember what we learned and when it was that we learned it… We've forgotten so much about the *whys*, that we'd probably be satisfied with just the *hows*. How did we get here, and what did it take? How did we come to our decisions, and were there any mistakes? How did we imagine our options would play out for us, and if there could ever be any retakes? If given the chance, these are the questions that we would ask of ourselves…the answers that we would get, we're sure we won't ever rightly know. Though, the quest for all that knowledge we imagine to be a worthwhile adventure. We won't rest until we know "who (we are)". At times, over the years, when life made sense, we were quite certain. Sometimes, in the quietest of moments, when there was no one to talk to, we weren't so sure. And, on a few occasions, with the noise of the world drowning out reason, we had no idea at all. So, in the mean time, between those moments, we look for someone who would "please tell (us)"… Is it that we're "sensible, logical, responsible (and) practical"? Could we also be "dependable, clinical, intellectual (and) cynical"? Would they call us "a radical, liberal, fanatical (maybe even) criminal"? Or, should we resolve to be "acceptable, respectable, (and) presentable, (like) a vegetable"? Whatever the case may be, and whatever they may say, and whatever answers we may find, we'll probably just keep on searching. No matter where we go, no matter what we do, and no matter who we're with, we'll still always and forever be ourselves. It's so "simple", but not so easy, to be exactly what we've become. We have to be who we are, at all times and forever, no matter what we want. Whatever the outcome, and whatever we need, we'll have to keep going on. It may sound "absurd" to some, maybe "the questions run (too) deep" for others, but for us to find ourselves is everything, and quite "logical"…

"Painted Sky" 2007

Conclusion

As we go through Life, it's not necessarily a matter of what we think, but how we feel that makes all the difference… When it comes time to decide, we hope we can remember what's most important. If there's a chance to reflect back on our moments, we should choose the good memories over the bad. As our sunrises turn into sunsets, we must welcome all forms of love, but no versions of hate. If we live each and every day on its own terms, we can be mindful of who we are, where we're going, and who we're with. Everything is so much easier when we give everyone, especially ourselves, a chance. The world is such a better place if we exist to the fullest and allow others to coexist. If only we could let the rhythms and rhymes of our planet guide us, we would be so much happier. For me, Rock 'n' Roll has been my soundtrack and backdrop. As I reflect back on my life, I know that I would be a different person without it. For all the people I have met, the things I have done, and the knowledge I have gained, each would've been framed in another way without the music. This is not to say that the music has made me, but it has helped *shape* me. If I can impart some of this wisdom onto others, then this work has not been in vain. I live each moment with the songs in my head, and I select just the right one from my playlist. Maybe you, too, can join me, or choose your own melodies to guide you… My sincerest desires, my deepest wishes, and my most heartfelt aspirations go out to everyone I know, those I haven't met yet, and the countless others whom I may never encounter… Arthur, Ruth, Helen, Ronit, Karen, Harry, Alex, Joe, and every one of my family and friends already know my feelings for them. To the rest of you, take my word for it and listen to what the songs in this book have to say. Life is what we make of it, how we look at it, and what we allow it to be for each and every one of us. Let us all be guided by these words as we journey through our lives striving for Harmony, Peace, and, especially, Love…

"Reflection" 1967

Printed in the United States
By Bookmasters